UP FROM METHODISM

UP
FROM
METHODISM

by

HERBERT ASBURY

THUNDER'S MOUTH PRESS ★ NEW YORK

UP FROM METHODISM

© 1926 by Alfred A. Knopf, Inc.
Foreword © 2003 by Roy Blount, Jr.

Published by
Thunder's Mouth Press
An Imprint of Avalon Publishing Group Incorporated
245 West 17th Street, 11th Floor
New York, NY 10011-5300

Library of Congress Catologing-in-Publication Data is available.

ISBN: 1-56025-570-6

9 8 7 6 5 4 3 2 1

DESIGNED BY PAULINE NEUWIRTH, NEUWIRTH & ASSOCIATES, INC.

Printed in the United States of America
Distributed by Publishers Group West

To Stanley Walker

CONTENTS

FOREWORD

Roy Blount Jr.

FEW PEOPLE have got more in the way of vocational inspiration out of church than Herbert Asbury, 1889-1963. The light he saw, though, was not the light intended. The hardshell Methodism Asbury grew up with in Farmington, Missouri, was all about sin — from harlotry to playing the phonograph on Sunday — and downright prodigal ways of repressing and suppressing it. "I was fallow ground for all these seeds of piety," he writes, "for I was a highly emotional and excitable boy."

A descendant of historically eminent Methodists, he did not, as expected, grow up to become a bishop. His attitude toward that prospect was neutral until the revival-service night in his teens when the church humiliated him— seduced him with music and induced him with tugs and shoves and heavy blandishment (he renders the experience almost as a gang-rape)—into coming tearfully forward unto the altar and offering his soul to salvation, when in his mind he knew he didn't mean it or want it. Thereafter, writes Asbury, he regarded religion "with a tongue in my cheek and a sneer in my heart." He became a newspaperman, which for many lapsed Methodists would have been louche enough, but in 1926 an excerpt from *Up From Methodism* made him scandalously famous.

Asbury sent this memoir of his youth to H.L. Mencken, whom he idolized. Mencken was taken by the chapter, "Hatrack," about Farmington's treatment of its outstanding fallen woman. The woman in question, called Hatrack because she was so scrawny, lay with men in fields of stone for small amounts of money. As a character she is young Asbury in reverse: she attends church longing to be saved, but the fold won't take her in (Perhaps because who then would fill her civic function). And so she sneers as he sneered, and turns herself out as the church did him. "Hatrack" appeared in Mencken's *American Mercury*, which delighted in mocking American sanctimony. The Watch and Ward society, whose civic function was to keep sin out of Boston, took one look at "Hatrack" and banned that issue. Mencken made a point of selling a copy, and being arrested for it, on the Boston Commons. Mencken had his landmark press freedom case—he won in court—and Asbury had his launch.

Within the year this book was published, and Asbury went on to a career of reveling, on paper, in sin. Most notably he authored dark-side histories of New York, New Orleans, San Francisco and Chicago. *The French Quarter: An Informal History of the New Orleans Underworld With Particular Reference to Its Colorful Iniquities* is the full title of the New Orleans one—on whose dust jacket Asbury's city-underworld series is summed up as follows: "These incredible accounts of violent life and violent death, and love both vile and violent, are as vivid as the red lights that sprinkled the streets he writes of." In 2002 Martin Scorsese adapted Asbury's *Gangs of New York* into a film about corruption and street fighting next to which the blue-nosed Methodism that soured Asbury's youth seems almost tolerable.

Mencken himself, who had never felt religiosity's siren appeal, made merrier sport of it. Herbie Asbury had been hurt by the church, and he was determined to show it a thing or two. And if he lacked some of what it takes to make a bishop, he had the balls: his take on holiness was brazen in the Twenties and remains so today. In fact, *Up From Methodism* sometimes reads like such a tract against religious hypocrisy that readers may wonder whether there isn't something to be said for it. Let it be said that Methodism began in Eighteenth-Century England as a socially conscious movement among the exploited working class, whose weakness for cheap gin and neglect of unplanned offspring the Church of England did not deign to address. When brought to the American heartland's shallow-rooted bourgeoisie – most pervasively by Herbert's collateral ancestor, Francis Asbury – the movement continued to lean hard on the evils of drunkenness and lust. In retrospect we may well feel that joylessness and impacted prurience were closer to home. But festering shame and dread did provide considerable prophylaxis — in the days before antibiotics, twelve-step programs and reliable birth control — against the wages of lower-class sin.

By the time I was growing up in and out of Methodism, half a century after Asbury, it had mellowed a great deal. (And today the United Methodist Church has officially opposed its most prominent adherent, President George W. Bush, for his administration's resort to war in Afghanistan and Iraq.) The church brought my parents together with life-long friends who, though abstinent, were much nicer, and jollier, than the churchfolk in this book. But the old devils lingered. The generation before me had known Methodism in something like the mode derided by Asbury, and never entirely got over it. As I grew more latitudinarian — under the influence of literature, the Sixties, and the sort of person that one meets (thank God) as a reporter — my parents and I lost the capacity to talk anything over civilly, much less jovially. My poor mother, whose childhood had been blighted by her father's early death from alcoholism and syphilis, was I believe terrified for me. If she didn't fear quite literally that I would, as Asbury puts it, "hang throughout eternity on a revolving spit over a great fire in the deepest pit of Hell, while little red devils jabbed white-hot pokers into my quivering flesh and Satan stood by and curled his lip in glee," she had no alternative vision for the posthumus years outside the church. And she found it unfathomable, I imagine, that I would adopt a way of thinking that precluded her seeing me in the life to come. There had to be a heaven, especially after my father died, because she had to see him there, and share the fountain of blessings that would justify her abstemious life on earth. I wanted to get around a bit while above ground. The gulf between her expectations shame.

"Blessed assurance, Jesus is mine. Oh, what a foretaste of glory divine." Those were some great old hymns, which Herbert Asbury loved in spite of himself and came to sing raucous parodies of. In them the church afforded a not entirely sublimated alternative to the more straightforward forms of intoxication and eroticism. Once in the Seventies I went, for journalistic reasons, to a church that had been turned into a dance club. People with spiked purple hair were prancing and dancing all over the pulpit. I hated it, because I could see my decent parents out there in their pew, needing to believe.

But there was also a ferocity in that worship, and traces of the cankering, perversely prideful self-denial that Herbert finds in the heritage of his holy forebear Francis, who wrote in his Journals: "I must lament that I am not perfectly cru-cified with God." Perhaps the most empathetic and the best sentence in *Up From Methodism* is Herbert's final judgment on Bishop Francis: "He yearned for a constant religious thrill, and mourned because he could not satisfy his yearning."

The inner Herbert Asbury, we get to know less well. A shade is drawn, whose nature may reside in the "tongue in my cheek" and the "sneer in my heart" that his suborned con-version left him with. Whom or what does he love? He may have relished the company of black Farmingtonians, but his way of using the term "darky" is unpleasantly flippant even allowing for standards of the time. I wish he had told us more about his vaguely sympathetic, not especially sanctified par-ents and siblings, who may have helped give him the gump-tion to strike out on his own. Or maybe his parents were too easy-going to be rebelled against, so he took on bigger game.

There is something less than wholly persuasive in his asser-tion, here in his mid-thirties, that "without religion I thor-oughly enjoy this business of living." He says he still doesn't like the taste of the booze he took up to spite the church. Whether he ever gave up the cigarettes that gave him bad-boy satisfaction, I don't know, but on the Internet (there is a her-bertasbury.com) we learn that after World War I, when he was gassed, he suffered for the rest of the life from pulmonary problems that eventually killed him. Most of his books, his chronicles of wickedness, he worked up from newspaper-morgue research. He never had the child that in this book he rather airily imagines exposing quite rationally to the world's religions. But he must have died secure in the belief that he had nailed (*pace* Bishop Francis) the people who imposed their sacred will upon him when he was vulnerable. There are lots of such people in the world today.

UP FROM METHODISM

CHAPTER I

HOME LIFE OF A BOY DESTINED FOR HEAVEN

1

ON MY father's side, according to my family belief, I am related to Cotton Mather; on my mother's side to Roger Williams. My great-great-uncle was Francis Asbury, the first Bishop of the Methodist Church to be ordained in America; his elder half-brother was my great-great-grandfather, Thomas Asbury, who, disowned by his father for various sins, ran away from the family cottage in England and went to sea. Later he kidnapped Susan Jennings and married her, and then settled in Virginia and so escaped the fate of the Bishop, who doubtless went to the Methodist Heaven.

My great-grandfather was the Rev. Daniel Asbury of Fairfax County, Va., an early pillar of Methodism and one of the great organizers of the Church in the South. When a young man he went to North Carolina, and in 1791 founded, in Lincoln County, the first Methodist church west of the Catawba River. Later he was a Presiding Elder and labored valiantly for the Wesleyan God. When but a boy he was captured by the Indians and kept a prisoner for several years, and is said to have converted the entire tribe to Christianity. Throughout his whole life Sunday was his great day—he was born on Sunday, converted on Sunday, captured by the Indians on Sunday, released on Sunday, reached home on Sunday, was ordained as a minister on Sunday, and on a Sunday married Nancy Morris in Brunswick County, Va. His first child was born on Sunday and he died on Sunday.

My grandfather was the Rev. William Asbury of North Carolina, a local preacher who, for some reason that I have never known, quit raising souls to Heaven and moved over into Mississippi, where he had equally poor success raising coons and cotton. He married Susan Lester Marks, member of an equally religious family. Several of his seven sons were Methodist preachers, and my father, too, would have assumed the cloth had not the Civil War come along. He enlisted in the Confederate Army and became an officer of infantry, and infantrymen do not make good preachers. At the close of the War he studied Civil Engineering and then moved to Missouri, and settled in Farmington, where I was born. He was county Surveyor of my home county of St. Francois for more than thirty years, and City Clerk of Farmington for twenty years. The exigencies of local politics compelled him to attend services and take an active part in church work, but I have no recollection of him as a religious man, although he imposed religion upon his home and impressed upon his family the necessity of Christian salvation.

I first suspected that he might not be as religious as reported when I whacked him across the shins with a broomstick as he sat in the yard one day nursing his rheumatism. He did not turn the other shin. This was not long after we had moved from the cottage across the street from the Masonic and Catholic cemeteries to our new house on the other side of the town, near the mansions of our first families, the Webers and the Cayces. Curiously enough, these graveyards were side by side, although their occupants presumably went to different Heavens. There was a high fence between them, and it was not easy to dispose of the border-line burial plots; the Protestants felt that a few Catholic demons might be able to crawl through or under the fence, and the Catholics did not wish to have their mortal remains so close to those of such benighted heathen as the Methodists and the Presbyterians.

My mother's people, the Prichards and the Blues, came originally from North Carolina, Georgia and Tennessee, and were for the most part devout Baptists, believing that in immersion alone was true salvation. The strength of their religious convictions may be seen in the fact that many of them never forgave my mother for marrying a Methodist and transferring her letter to my father's Church, forsaking the austerities of her family faith. They considered the Methodists too liberal! The true baptist of those days was in a constant emotional upheaval; his religion was a canker that ate deeper and deeper, and he was able to find no relief; the more religious he became, the more miserable he was. On the other hand, the Methodist enjoyed terrific and periodical emotional explosions, and thereafter was generally able to live for a few days in comparative calm. But the Baptist was wrapped in gloom from the moment of his conversion until he was called home to Jesus.

When my mother's forbears came up from the South they settled within a radius of twenty miles of Farmington, many of them in the vicinity of Hazel Run and French Village. They were farmers, with a sprinkling of small storekeepers, preachers and country doctors. My mother's father, Joseph Prichard, was a farmer, but he was very religious and was renowned throughout the countryside around French Village for his exploits as a faith healer; he could cure toothache, remove warts and stop the flow of blood. His method was merely to say: "It will be gone by the time you get home," and generally it was. He frequently removed warts from my own hands; at least they vanished within a reasonable time after he had looked at them and pronounced his incantations, and I regarded him with awe.

There was a tradition in our family that my grandfather boasted Indian blood in his veins, and although I do not think it was true, at the time it gave me great pride and satisfaction; it invested me with authority at such times as we played Indian and Wild West games. He made a two-year trip overland to California during the 1849 gold rush, without conspicuous success, and brought back with him the musket with which we were given to understand he had slain innumerable Indians. Two or three times a year his children and his grandchildren, a vast horde all told, held family reunions at his French Village farm, and the big moment of the day came in the afternoon when all of the grandchildren trooped into the woods behind the barn to watch Grandpa kill a squirrel. We stood in a half-circle, almost overcome by awe, while my grandfather loaded his gun with great care, pouring the correct amount of powder from his powder horn and dumping the bullets from his pouch into the palm of his hand, where he counted them carefully. And then he killed the squirrel, while we stood behind him and marveled. He never failed; he was an excellent rifle shot; in his ninety-first year, three years before he died, he knocked a squirrel from a tree as easily as Davy Crockett could have done it.

As a young man in Georgia and later in Missouri my grandfather Prichard was famous as a leader of Baptist singsongs. His favorite hymn was "The Prodigal Son," which he was wont to bellow with fanatical fervor as he sat bolt upright in an uncomfortable, straight-backed chair and directed the singing with a stick. He sang from an old hymn book which had been in his family for many years, a curious volume with the music printed in square notes. Many of the hymns expressed sentiments that to-day, even in religious circles, would be considered obscene. I recall one that said: "Oh, sinners! My bowels do move with desire!"

I was constantly under the influence of my mother's people, who did what they could to overcome the pernicious influence of the Methodists; they prevailed upon me to visit them and attend their revivals and other religious meetings, and otherwise attempted to oversee and assure my eventual salvation. Some of my father's people, too, had come up from the South, from Virginia and North Carolina and Mississippi, and had settled around Farmington. Many of them were excessively pious, although it is my recollection that they did not carry their love of God and man into the conduct of their temporal affairs; religion was not permitted to interfere with business. Between them and my mother's people there was a constant, although not open, fight for my soul, and the souls of my sister and brothers. The bout appears to have been a draw.

2

WE were a musical family. My elder brother and I played the harmonica, or French harp, as we called it then, and my sister performed capably upon the organ, the guitar and the mandolin. She was particularly adept upon the guitar, and enjoyed an enviable reputation for the way she whanged out the fandango pieces and the tune descriptive of the Battle of Sebastopol, which requires much banging and thumping and difficult fingering. My father was a fiddler. He did not know one note from another, but he could tuck his fiddle under his chin, tap the floor with his foot and play with great spirit such tunes as "Fisher's Hornpipe," "Billy in the Low Ground," "Turkey in the Straw" and "The Arkansas Traveler." But his muse was dumb if he could not pat his foot. I could also beat a snare drum passably, and later I learned to play the violin, the cornet and the alto horn, so that we had quite a family orchestra, and our house was frequently filled with music. Anyhow we played these instruments.

But not on Sunday. Our Preacher assured us that music on Sunday, except in church, was sinful and an affront to the Heavenly Father, and on Saturday night, after a final orgy of melody, my mother gathered up the guitars and mandolins, the fiddles, the drums and the harmonicas and all of the other musical instruments, even the Jew's-harp, and put them under lock and key until Monday morning. We could not even play a comb on Sunday, although on rare occasions, usually when the Preacher was there and gave permission and absolution from sinful consequences, I was permitted to bring out my big harmonica, from which I could produce the sonorous tones of an organ, and play church hymns such as "Rock of Ages" and "Nearer, My God, to Thee." But I was forbidden to play "Turkey in the Straw" or "The Mocking Bird" with variations. The latter was my favorite tune, because by jiggling my hand over the harmonica I could produce a very effective trill which I fondly believed was as beautiful as the singing of a canary, but if I launched into such a tune on Sunday I had debauched the Sabbath, and my harmonica was taken from me. And frequently I myself was taken into the woodshed and taught a proper respect for the Lord's Day.

Under no circumstances could we play the fiddle in our house on Sunday, because of all music, that which came from the fiddle was the most sinful. It was the Devil's instrument. No fiddling on Sunday had been a cardinal rule of my father's family since Colonial days in Virginia, and later in Mississippi and in North Carolina my grandmother had compelled her Negro slaves to put up their musical instruments from Saturday night to Monday morning. Eventually I took lessons from the music teacher in Farmington and learned to call the fiddle a violin, and as I grew older I played when I pleased, although not very successfully. But so long as the instrument remained a fiddle it was played in our house on Sunday on only one occasion. And then the performance was a neighborhood scandal, and only the fact that the instrument had been played by a Preacher saved us from getting into trouble with God and His representatives in Farmington.

This tweaking of the heavenly nose occurred during a District Conference, when the visiting preachers were parceled out among the faithful of the local Methodist church. Two came to us, one a young man filled with good works and a constant, fretful worry over the low estate of the human race, and the other an old man who had been a wicked sinner in his time and who had never been able to resist an occasional temptation to have a good time. He was a Virginian and an accomplished fiddler, but he could play nothing but dance music, which the darkies had taught him. The first Sunday they were at our house my father admitted that we had a fiddle, and the old Preacher demanded that it be brought out for him to perform upon. My father and mother were in terror all afternoon for fear that the neighbors would hear the wailing of the fiddle, although they prevailed upon the old man to use a mute and the music could hardly be heard outside the room. We were particularly afraid that a devout Sister, who lived next door to us and whose principal occupation was going to church, might hear it; if she had it would have been nothing short of a catastrophe, for the tale would have been all over town before nightfall. So we closed the windows and the doors, muted the fiddle and put the old Preacher in the parlor, where he fiddled until he had sinned enough. But even then several people passing along the street heard it, and I do not think that we ever quite lived it down. We could convince no one that the fiddle had been played by a Man of God. Everyone knew better; Men of God did not do such things.

3

EVERY Wednesday night we attended prayer meeting, and on Sundays we went to Sunday school and twice to church. And on Sunday afternoon, and on week days, there were the sessions of the various church organizations. We had grace before meat in our home, and when the Preacher came to dinner he delivered long-winded prayers on the universal theme of "gimme." We did not have that emotional orgy called family prayer, but I did not escape it; I encountered it in many

Farmington homes and in the houses of almost all of my relatives.

It was particularly oppressive in the home of an oppressively devout kinsman whom I called uncle. He was not actually my uncle; he was related to my father by marriage, and I do not believe there was any blood kinship, but I thought of him as uncle, and he had a certain measure of authority over me, so that to a considerable extent I was under his control and subject to his influence until I became intelligent enough to have an occasional thought of my own.

My uncle was an extraordinarily pious man, an official of our church and of our Sunday school, and a leader in every movement designed to entice the sinner from his wicked ways and lead him to the true religion of the Wesleyans. He was intent upon salvation for everyone, and let no opportunity pass to serve the Lord. He frowned upon laughter, and although he had a very charming family, there was little joy in his home; a laugh seemed to make him uncomfortable and start a train of dismal religious thought, and I gathered the impression that all mirth was a direct and studied affront to God.

Every night after dinner, or supper, as we called it then, his living room was given over to family prayer. I frequently spent the night with his youngest son, my chum for many years, and was compelled to attend with the others and absorb my nightly dose of religion, and listen to a solemn account of the fearful things that God would do to us if we strayed from the path of righteousness. There was no laughter, and there were no jokes; the whole atmosphere of the house turned gray and gloomily oppressive when my uncle rose from his seat, glanced sorrowfully at his family, and announced:

"We will now have prayers."

He turned and with bowed head passed into the living room. We sat at the supper table for a moment in silence, myself seeing goblins and fearsome avenging creatures of God leering at me from every shaded corner of the room, and my mind racing madly over the day's activities to discover what I had done that required an alibi. In a few moments my aunt arose and went slowly into the other room, and then one by one the others. We marched solemnly, with downcast eyes; we might have been going to a funeral. Indeed, it seems to me now that we must in truth have been going to a funeral; here was a fine house built for the warmth of human happiness, turned into a forbidding mausoleum by the mere mention of God.

In the living room Uncle awaited us, standing beside the small table on which, always, there was nothing but the Family Bible. He waited in silence until we had taken our places, and then he laid reverent hands upon the Book and began fumbling with the pages, glancing sharply over his spectacles to make sure that everyone was undergoing some sort of emotional upheaval, and looking particularly for some sign of revolt from his son and myself. I doubt if he ever knew it, but when I attended family prayer in his house I did not think of revolt. I was in an agony of fright; I felt as if something was crushing me, and that something was my uncle's God, an avenging monster ready to devour me for my sins. God was in the house and I was afraid.

The most uncomfortable chairs in the house were used for family prayer, and we perched upon their edges, afraid to sink back and relax, because we had been told many times that discomfort and righteousness were well-nigh synonymous. God would have been scandalized and indignant had we made ourselves comfortable to listen to His Word. And then my uncle read from the Bible. He read without joy; he held in his hand the Book which in his eyes was the sole hope of humanity, the Book that contained the glad news that for all mankind there was salvation, but he read it as if it were a sentence of death, slowly and solemnly, dwelling with horrible clarity upon those phrases that promised punishment. The Bible seemed to have no effect upon him but to make him gloomy and miserable.

At the conclusion of his reading, he slowly closed the Bible and placed it upon the table. He then stood for a moment in profound thought, his chin resting upon his breast. I assumed that he was overcome by contemplation of the sins of a wicked world. Those of us who were young began about this time to itch with that devilish itch which invariably afflicts a youngster when there is a penalty for scratching. We itched and itched, but we were afraid to scratch because God was in the room, and we knew as well as we knew anything that He would punish us if we moved. And finally my uncle stared at the ceiling and said:

"Let us pray."

With almost the precision of automata we knelt by our chairs, our knees grinding into the hard carpet, while my uncle's voice soared in a sonorous appeal to the Lord to give us some of this and some of that, to bless us and make us prosperous, and, in effect, to hell with such infidels as Jews, Catholics and Presbyterians. And then he rose slowly to his feet and passed from the room, without speaking. We followed, and scattered about our various affairs, but it was a long time before we could shake off the effects of the religious debauch and play with any zest. And nearly always I awoke some hours later in the throes of a nightmare, pursued by fiends and demons shrieking that I was to be boiled and fried and cooked in the fires of Hell.

Every night year after year this sort of thing went on in houses all over Farmington, and for that matter all over the United States. It would be interesting to know how many hours were wasted in the course of a year by such senseless appeals to the Heavenly Father, by this constant reiteration of "gimme, gimme, gimme."

4

MANY of my relatives on my mother's side attended Colony Church, about three miles from Farmington. This was a hard-shell Baptist congregation, the members of which took their religion with the utmost seriousness and were constantly on the lookout for sin to rear its reptile head. If it did they assailed it with glad cries. There was no organ in this church; indeed, for many years none of the Baptist churches in and about Farmington would permit any sort of music at their services, holding that music was an invention of the Devil designed to entice Christians from respectful contemplation of the mercies and graces of the Lord, and that no devout Christian could hear music and still keep his mind on God and his heart true to the faith. Their attitude toward the organ was exactly that of the good Sister of whom Will Carleton sang in his Farm ballads:

> I've been a Sister good and true
> For five and thirty year;
> I've done what seemed my part to do,
> And prayed my duty clear.
> But death will stop my voice, I know,
> For he is on my track;
> And some day I to church will go,

And nevermore come back.
And when the folks get up to sing,
    Whene'er that time shall be—
I do not want no patent thing,
    A-squealin' over me.

In later years, of course, the Baptists became almost civilized and most of their churches bought organs; in some there were even pianos. But in few of the churches of the Farmington countryside, in my early youth, was there more fervent religion on tap than at Colony Church. There were frequent revivals, and many basket dinners, when the farm women brought huge quantities of food to the church early in the morning, and all day long the congregation gave itself up to an orgy of eating and saving souls. At most of these revivals there were foot-washings; they were usually announced at the morning service for the afternoon, and then there was a great scurrying home or to the nearest creek, or crick, as it was generally called, where the feet were washed vigorously with soap and made presentable for public exposure in the aisles and around the pulpit of the church.

One of the most famous of the Colony Church foot-washings, one that is still talked about when the good Brothers and Sisters get together in that neighborhood, ended the enmity of a widow, Sister Letts, and a lawyer whose name I do not recall. For years there had been great bitterness between them, and although the congregation had prayed for them and had exhorted them to forgive, the Lord had not entered their hearts, and so they continued to treasure their hate. But at length, on a Sunday morning during a revival, the preacher announced that there would be a foot-washing that afternoon, and the Brother rose and spoke:

"I have opened my heart to God," he said, "and He has

instructed me to forgive Sister Letts. This afternoon I shall wash her feet."

There was a murmur of enthusiasm all over the church, and one leather-lunged Brother popped to his feet and shouted: "Amen, Brother! Glory to God!" And then Sister Letts bounced to her feet and cried that she, too, praised the Lord and would wash the feet of the Brother.

That afternoon the church was crowded. Almost every family of the countryside was on hand to see God end this bitter quarrel which had come so near to disrupting the congregation. The service proceeded as usual, opening with some such catchy hymn as "Bringing in the Sheaves," and then through the sermon to the slow, solemn songs like "How Firm a Foundation" and "Nearer, My God, to Thee." Then came the foot-washing, when the Brothers and Sisters proved their humility and showed that when it came right down to brass tacks they were no better than Jesus Christ. It was felt that the legal Brother and Sister Letts should have the honor thus to show off first before God, and so for a little while no one moved when the Preacher announced that the time had come, and that basins of water and towels would be provided.

But at length the Brother got to his feet and marched stiffly down the aisle to the pulpit, where he procured a pan and a towel. With these in hand he paraded back up the aisle toward the last row, where Sister Letts rocked back and forth and murmured in ecstasy:

"Praise the Lord, Brother! Praise the Lord!"

Moving slowly to a chorus of amens and unintelligible mumblings of piety, the Brother was some distance up the aisle when Sister Letts started to meet him. Halfway between the back door and the pulpit they stopped, facing each other.

And then a new difficulty arose. They had by now thoroughly given themselves to God and were suffused with a wonderful glow of self-appreciation at this proof of their humility, but each wanted to prove it first. Each appeared to feel that the one who first washed a foot would receive the greater amount of kudos from the Lord.

So they began to argue, and the heat of the discussion spread all over the congregation, and here and there Brothers and Sisters became so upset by the spirit that they jumped to their feet and began shouting loudly, bouncing up and down and flinging their arms about. My sister, a small child, was practically overcome by curiosity, and added to the excitement by leaning too far from her seat and falling into the aisle, so eager was she to see the ceremony. She was promptly spanked and put back in place by my Aunt Ophelia, and several devout persons near her intimated strongly that she was a sinful, blasphemous little wretch.

It seemed for a time that there would be a deadlock, as neither Sister Letts nor the Brother was willing to give in. So the congregation sang a hymn while they stood staring at each other, and then the Preacher prayed to the Lord to make a decision as to who should wash whose feet first. And apparently God said Eeney Meeney Miney Mo and picked Sister Letts to be It, for the Brother suddenly surrendered and sat in a chair which had been pushed into the aisle for him. He bared his foot, and Sister Letts dropped to her knees and poked it into the basin of water. I do not know if the Brother wriggled his toes. Having laved him, Sister Letts plied her towel vigorously to a groaning chorus of "Amen!" that arose from all parts of the church, and then she sat in the chair and removed her shoe and stocking and the Brother performed the ceremony. The congregation, everyone filled to the bursting point with emotion, then stood and sang quaveringly "How Firm a Foundation." Sister Letts and the Brother returned to their seats. It was generally agreed that by washing each other's feet they had practically assured themselves choice seats in Heaven.

5

I was fallow ground for all these seeds of piety, for I was a highly emotional and excitable boy. I wept when I heard slow music, I shivered with fear over the ghost stories and the frightful tales of Hell that were told to me with such regularity, and it was usually I who saw the spooks when we played or hunted for bumblebees among the tombs of the Masonic cemetery. There is no telling what I might have seen had I ever been able to summon sufficient courage to enter the Catholic cemetery at night. I did go as far as just inside the gate once, and immediately there arose in front of me an apparition that to my mind could be nothing less than the Devil himself. And this was not surprising, for I well knew that the Catholics were worshipers of a false God, and it was quite likely that their graveyard was the abode of evil spirits.

Because of my temperament, which impelled me to believe everything I was told, and because from time to time I had shown indications of being a bad boy if restraint were not exercised, I received more religious instruction than my sister or my brothers. Again, there was the matter of ancestry. Our family connections, especially my father's people, were very proud of our relationship to the Bishop and our direct descent from the Rev. Daniel Asbury, and they settled on me to carry on the family tradition. There was much talk of sending me to a theological school, and I appeared to be destined for the Church, so that I was always waiting for the call to preach, though conscious of a vague hope that it would be delayed.

But I had no idea that I should escape such a fate, for I accepted as a basic fact of life that in every generation at least one Asbury should be a Methodist preacher. Wherever I went I encountered the assumption that I was to succeed the Bishop and the Presiding Elder, and become a Methodist Messiah howling in the wilderness of sin and shoving souls into the heavenly hoppers with both hands. Everyone seemed to take it for granted, and when I talked to a stranger he invariably said:

"Well, well! So your name is Asbury?"

"Yes, sir."

"Kin to the Bishop?"

"Yes, sir."

"Well, well! I suppose you will be a preacher, too?"

"Yes, sir. I guess so."

If the person to whom I talked was himself a Preacher, or a Brother, he would smile gently, pat my head with a moist palm and say: "God bless you, my boy," and pad on down the street. I can recall but one person who did not make some such senseless remark. He was a hardware drummer from St. Louis, a fat, waggish person in flashy raiment, doubtless a sinner, who stopped me as I marched proudly past Doss's barber shop carrying a string of fish, one of which was as large a bass as was ever taken out of the St. Francis River. He tried to buy the big fish, and when I refused to sell he asked me my name and the inevitable conversation followed. But when I said to him: "Yes, sir, I guess so," he wrinkled his nose and said: "Don't be a damned fool, kid."

I felt a sudden rush of affection for this outspoken person, although I shuddered at the thought of what would happen to him if a Preacher or a Brother heard him using profanity and told God about it. I proffered him one of my string, a fine crappie, which he accepted gratefully and on which he feasted later at the St. Francis Hotel. Later in the evening I met him as he swung blithely through the doors of Perringer's Saloon, and he jovially invited me in to have a glass of beer. I thought he must be crazy; I would no more have entered a saloon then than I would have committed mayhem upon the Preacher. In later life, of course, I did enter saloons, but have never been able to bring myself to bite a preacher, although at times I have been sorely tempted. But it was a long time before I understood what the drummer meant when he said, as we parted:

"Well, look out, kid, and don't let them put that Bishop stuff over on you."

CHAPTER II

THE MACHINERY OF
SALVATION

FARMINGTON WAS about eight or ten miles from the lead-
mining district of Southeast Missouri, where a great number
of low foreigners were employed, but God did not permit any
ore to be found near us and so kept our town holy and unde-
filed by their presence. We did not greatly concern ourselves
with their evil ways, because we knew that foreigners were little if any better than the beasts of the field, and that God had
put them on earth for some inscrutable purpose of His own,
with which we were not to meddle. Even the Preachers and
the amateur devil-chasers in such towns as Flat River and
Bonne Terre devoted their activities principally to spreading
the Gospel among the home-bred and let the Hunkies carry

on whatever nefarious practices pleased them best. We didn't want them in our Heaven, anyhow.

Our town nestled in the foothills of the Ozarks, some eighty-six miles from St. Louis and two miles from the DeLassus station on the Belmont branch of the Iron Mountain Railroad. But the civilizing influences of the city seldom touched any of us except a few wealthy families who could afford the railroad fare for frequent trips. We had then some 2,500 inhabitants, the vast majority of whom were devout workers for the Protestant God, especially on Sunday. During the week many of them put sand in the sugar and weighed their thumbs with the sausage, and otherwise engaged in legitimate and profitable business enterprise, but on Sunday they praised the Lord.

There were but two or three Jewish families in town then, and I do not recall that they ever attempted to practice their religion; certainly not in public. Doubtless our God would have destroyed them if they had thus flaunted their sin in our faces, and mocked us with their heathen rites. It is my recollection that they attended the Presbyterian church, but if so it was for business or social reasons. The Catholics had a church, but they were not numerically strong, and did not amount to a great deal in the town's scheme of things, although they occasionally captured a city office or did a bit of proselyting among the backsliders of the Protestant congregations. They labored earnestly one whole summer trying to ensnare my sister after her allegiance to the Methodist Father had wavered, but they were unsuccessful. She could not swallow the Pope, or the holy images and the like. Nor could she learn to cross herself properly, although I became much interested and helped her; we used to go behind the barn and practice in all seriousness, but we invariably found ourselves giggling at the rite. And few things can destroy religion quicker than a hearty giggle.

The Protestants of Farmington made little if any effort to induce the Catholics to abandon their debaucheries and embrace the true religion; generally we considered them benighted heathens and crazy people and let it go at that, confident that in due time God would blast them with His wrath, destroy their churches and perhaps send their young women to Heaven to be virgin angels in a Protestant paradise. I was very eager to see this wholesale destruction, and waited patiently for many years, hoping that God would furnish advance information to His intimate, our Methodist pastor, so we would be able to view the performance. I strongly favored an earthquake and a bolt of lightning, as being more spectacular. But I am sorry to say that nothing ever happened, although one night lightning struck the steeple of the Catholic church and there was some talk about town that God was limbering up His muscles and getting ready to show what He could really do.

Some of our most advanced thinkers conceded that perhaps the Catholics and the few nondescripts who professed religion for the sake of business but who would not attend church, had their own God, quite different from ours and unquestionably a very inferior Deity. But people who held this view were considered entirely too charitable; it was all right to admit that God might, in the fullness of time, and out of that loving mercy which keeps half the world constantly at the throats of the other half, relent and permit a few Catholics to enter Heaven as low menials, but to say that they might have a Heaven of their own was going a bit too far. Both socially and spiritually they were on the other side of the railroad tracks. They were simply not in our set, and when any of them attended our parties, as sometimes happened despite every precaution, it was a matter of very great concern. Things may be different now, but when I was a boy cringing before the threatening lash of the Methodist God, there was grave doubt that anyone who lived south of the Post Office would ever amount to anything spiritually.

All of the reigning sects of the Protestants had churches in our town. There was also a Lutheran Church somewhere down by Schramm's Ice Plant, but its congregation was made up of Germans and what not, who ranked scarcely higher than the Catholics and the Jews. For some time during my final year in high school I was devotedly attached to a young Lutheran girl, and this attachment was the cause of considerable concern among some of my relatives. It was, then, my intention to marry her, although I quickly abandoned it after I had tentatively broached the matter to one of my aunts.

"She is not a Christian girl," my aunt protested.

"She is a Lutheran," I said. "They are Protestants."

"But some of their services are in German! How can they be Christians?"

She was perfectly sincere. She believed firmly that God understood no language but English, and that, having no knowledge of German, He could not look with favor upon a Lutheran. But it developed that this particular Lutheran could not look with favor upon a Methodist, which was probably an insult to our Methodist God. It was a great many years before I overcame my surprise that God did not do something about it, yet He seems to have done nothing but make her happy and her husband prosperous.

Most of the churches in our town were on Columbia Street, the principal thoroughfare, and they and their subsidiary schools were so numerous that we proudly called

Farmington "The City of Schools and Churches," and enjoyed great renown throughout Southeast Missouri for municipal piety and Christian education. On this street worshiped the Presbyterians, the Southern Methodists—this was the church of the Asburys and enjoyed special favors from the Lord—the Northern Methodists, and the Christians or Campbellites. The Baptists had a church in another part of town, in Doss's Addition. Each of these churches had a great many interlocking organizations, including Home Missionary Societies, Foreign Missionary Societies, Ladies' Aid Societies and other holy groups.

The Ladies' Aid Societies of the Middle West have become famous, and they deserve their renown. When I was a boy they were in truth most noble organizations. They rotated their meetings at the homes of the members, performing at each house about once every two weeks, according to the number of women who belonged. Their sessions were excessively sanctimonious; they opened and closed with prayer, and frequently some good Sister would at other times feel the spirit of the Lord working within her, and she would pop up from the quilting frame or the shirt on which she was sewing for the heathen and yelp an appeal to God to give her something or damn somebody. There were also Bible-readings at these meetings; in fact every time a member of our church called on another member, a verse from the Bible was read and a prayer was offered. And curiously enough these devout Christian Sisters displayed a greater liking for the books of the Old Testament than for those of the New.

In all of our congregations there were many special societies for young people, to which the children of the godly had to belong and whose meetings they had to attend. Their number was great, and the majority of their titles escape me, but I recall such outfits as the Christian Endeavor, the Loyal Temperance Legion, the Epworth League, the Baptist Young People's Union, and the Sunshine Brigade. The Legion was a union organization of juvenile foes of rum, and we used to meet on Sunday afternoons in the Presbyterian or Southern Methodist church and hear lectures on the evils of drink, after which we would stand, raise our right hands and shout in unison:

> We hate Rum!
> We hate Rum!
> We hate Rum!
> Our bodies will never be ravaged by drink!

The Sunshine Brigade was another union organization, in which all of the churches combined, and was composed of boys from eight to twelve or thirteen years of age. We met two or three times a week, in the evening after supper, generally on the spacious lawn of Merrifield Huff, the lawyer, and first we heard a Bible-reading and a prayer. Then we drilled, in military fashion, under the command of older boys who had been away to military schools. Then there were more verses from the Bible, another prayer, and we were sent home with unctuous commands to be good boys and think often of the mercy of the Lord. They called us "Little Soldiers of the Lord," and "Our Group of Manly Little Fellows." There was nothing we could do about it.

The activities of the Epworth League and the Baptist Young People's Union are too well known to require comment; they persist to this day, and there seems to be no likelihood that the present generation will make an intellectual advance sufficient to laugh them out of existence. Fortunately Farmington was spared the Young Men's Christian Association, and I had no contacts with that remarkable agency of salvation until I went to France with the American Army. Of my many encounters with the Y. M. C. A. abroad, two stand out in my memory. One occurred when I wanted a toothbrush, while in command of a platoon of infantry in the support line on the Vesle river front, between Fismes and Bazoches. I walked the eight miles or so back to division headquarters with a five-franc note in my pocket, all the money I had in the world.

The Y. M. C. A. canteen was open there, and after the secretary in charge had greeted me sweetly as Brother and inquired after the condition of my immortal soul, he produced a toothbrush, for which he wanted two francs, then about forty cents. I said I would buy it, there being no Red Cross hut near where I could have got one for nothing, and laid down my five-franc note. But the Y. M. C. A. man could not change it, nor could we find anybody else around headquarters who could do so. The Y man said that he could not let me have the toothbrush without payment and put it back in the case, and I walked the eight miles back to my command without it, rejecting his offer of a free pocket Bible with the observation that the line was one hell of a place for a Bible.

The second encounter with the Y. M. C. A. occurred a week or so later, at La Pres Farm, on the same front and on the road between Mont St. Martin and Chery Chartreuve. I had about two hundred sick and flat-footed infantrymen there, waiting for gas masks and other equipment so they could be moved to the front, and they had nothing to smoke. Neither did they have any money, because they had not been paid for months. To the farm came a Y. M. C. A. man laden with boxes, and when I asked him what they were, he said cigars. He showed them to my platoon sergeant and myself; they were fine, fat, handsome smokes.

I suggested that he lay out his stock, and that I would have the sergeant march the troops past in columns of twos, so that each man could have a cigar.

"That's fine," said the Y man, "they're fifteen-cent cigars, but the boys can have them for ten cents."

I told him that to my knowledge there was not ten cents in the whole outfit, and suggested that he give the cigars to the soldiers and look to Heaven for payment. But he would not; he said that he had brought the cigars to the line to sell and that he had to have the money for them. So I did the thing that seemed best under the circumstances. I took his cigars away from him, the sergeant headed him for Division Headquarters, and I kicked him as hard as I could in the pants. The last I saw of him, he was stumbling down the hill toward the crossroad vowing vengeance. But I paid little attention to him; I was busy handing out free cigars, and a few minutes later everybody at the farm was puffing happily.

We had also in Farmington three denominational schools, Elmwood Seminary, a girl's college with primary and grammar departments for both sexes, operated by the Presbyterians across the street from their church; Carleton College in the lower end of the town, a Northern Methodist institution; and Baptist College, near the Baptist church. Carleton and Baptist were coeducational. I was educated—God save the mark!—at Elmwood and Carleton, and at both there was much emphasis on religious teaching. Carleton, of course, since it was run by the Northern Methodists, was frankly a mill for grinding out workers for the Lord, and they poured out of the hopper in large numbers for many years. Gawky country boys came from the farms around Bull Run, Hazel

Run and French Village, and down-state toward Libertyville and Fredericktown, and entered Carleton College, to emerge a few years later rip-snorting evangelists hot on the trail of the Devil. Those who did not become professional Satan-chasers developed, in the course of time, into pussyfooting Brothers with keen ears for scandal, gimlet eyes for boring searchingly and suspiciously into all amusement and pleasure, and wagging tongues for scattering seeds of holiness. And God made their teeth very sharp, for backbiting.

Curiously enough, the Presbyterians in Farmington comprised the liberal element, in so far as we had a liberal element. This was because our wealthy families, or at least our social leaders, were apparently Episcopalians at heart and perhaps belonged to the Presbyterian congregation only because we had no Episcopal church. They were able to go to St. Louis frequently, and did, and consequently acquired a bit of metropolitan polish, and rubbed off some of our small-town intolerance and roughness. From time to time rumors were afloat that some of these people had been seen entering Episcopal churches in St. Louis, but I have never heard that they were verified.

But for many years this element had a virtual monopoly on such sinful practices as playing cards, dancing and buggy-riding on the Sabbath. I have heard several Brothers and Sisters, and more than one doleful and sorrowing Preacher, speak regretfully of the unholy spectacle of a young man of one of these families driving a spanking pair through the heart of the town on Sunday afternoon, with an abandoned young woman beside him and neither apparently caring one single damn about the fate of religion. It was prophesied that they could come to no good end. But the germ they planted multiplied enormously.

CHAPTER III

TABOOS OF THE LORD'S DAY

1

SUNDAY SHOULD be a day of gladness, and of light and beauty, for it is then that the forthright religionist is closest to his God, and when he is, if ever, in communion with the Holy Spirit and presumably receives instruction with which to confound the wicked during the ensuing week. But in small communities which suffer from the blight of religion it never is, and when I was a boy in Farmington Sunday was a day of dreadful gloom; over everything hung an atmosphere of morbid fear and dejection. In the morning the whole town donned its Sunday suit, almost always black and funereal and depressing, and therefore becoming to religious practice, and trudged sorrowfully and solemnly to Sunday School and to church, there to wail doleful hymns and hear an unlearned man "measure with words the immeasurable and sink the string of thought into the fathomless;" and beseech the Lord upon the universal prayer theme of "gimme." Then the village marched, in mournful cadence, back home for Sunday dinner. But before the meal was eaten the juvenile members of the religious household were commanded to remove their sabbath raiment, and were not again permitted to assume the habiliments of the godly until after supper, when the family clutched its Bibles and wandered forth despairingly to evening service.

These excursions, with attendance upon the various meetings of the young people's societies and other church organizations, comprised almost the sum total of the Sunday activity of our town's inhabitants. In recent years the young folks there appear to have gone wholeheartedly to the Devil, and are gallivanting about the country in automobiles, listening to radios, dancing, attending baseball games on the Sabbath and otherwise disporting themselves in a sinful manner, but in my youth we had to observe a very definite list of Sunday taboos, in addition to the special don'ts laid down by the more devout families, according to their fear of God and the fervor of their belief.

We could not play card games on Sunday. Regulation playing cards of course, were taboo at all times in the best and most religious families, for God, we were told, had informed the Preacher that cards were an invention of the Devil, designed to lure true believers into sin; but on Sunday we could not even play such games as Lotto, Old Maid and Authors. On week days these were considered very amusing and instructive pastimes, although in some quarters it was felt that they caused too much laughter, but if anyone so much as thought of them on Sunday he was headed for Hell.

The taboo against drinking was in effect every day in the week for the godly and their children, not on account of the possible harmful physical effects of liquor, but because God objected. And even the Town Sot hesitated to take a drink on Sunday, for he knew that every Preacher and every Brother and Sister would be howling to God to damn his immortal soul and make a horrible example out of him. And how they did love horrible examples!

No indoor games were permitted. This taboo was in force against "Drop-the-Handkerchief," "Puss-in-the-Corner," "Ring-Around the Rosy," and "London Bridge is Falling Down;" in fact, it included everything the Preacher could think of except games founded on the Bible. That is, we could play games in which questions of Biblical history were asked and answered, but they had to be conducted in a very solemn and decorous manner. At the first laugh, or at the first question based on the more ribald portions of the Scriptures, such as Numbers and Deuteronomy, the game was stopped and everyone went home in disgrace. One of my young friends who once asked what happened to Laban's household idol was soundly thrashed, as was another who requested a young lady to enumerate the ingredients of Ezekiel's bread. The curious may learn what the Holy Prophet ate by consulting Ezekiel 4:15.

We could have no outdoor games; in many families, indeed, it was considered irreligious to go out of doors at all except to church. Restless boys were sometimes permitted to walk around the block, and once in a great while to play, if they did so quietly and remained in the back yard, where, presumably, the Lord could not see them. Anyhow, the neighbors couldn't.

Parties and teas were forbidden, and we could not visit on Sunday, as a general rule, except among relatives. And such visits were usually turned into holy sing-songs, but since most of the hymns were either pornographic or slightly Sadistic, there were thrills galore in this sort of thing.

Walking along the main street of the town on Sunday was a sin of the first magnitude. Occasionally a group would obtain permission to stroll sedately down to Old Maid's Springs and take kodak pictures in a refined and genteel manner, but a young man and a girl caught ambling along Columbia street were the objects of much unfavorable comment. It was generally agreed that they were no better than they should be, and often a Preacher, or a Brother or Sister, would stop them and order them to cease desecrating the Lord's Day by such frivolous conduct.

"Go home," they would be told, "and pray to God to forgive you."

We could not go buggy riding on Sunday until we were old enough to take our hope of the hereafter in our hands and tacitly admit our allegiance to Satan. Girls who did so and thus flaunted their sin were ostracised by many of our best families, and were regarded as abandoned hussies, if not scarlet women. A man had to hold a good many promissory notes for his daughter to get away with a thing like that.

The Lord did not approve of Sunday night suppers, and so we could not have them. In the homes of the godly there was only a cold snack for the evening meal. It was considered sinful to light a fire in the cook-stove after twelve o'clock noon. One woman who moved to Farmington from St. Louis had the brazen audacity to give formal Sunday night dinners, but she scandalized the town and nobody would attend but a few Episcopalians disguised as Presbyterians. And even they could not bring themselves to wear evening clothes. But God soon punished her; she was so severely criticised that she finally went back to the city.

Dancing on Sunday, of course, or for that matter on any other day, was the Sin of Sins. I was told, and until I was almost grown believed it, that whoever danced on the Sabbath would immediately be engulfed in a wave of Heavenly wrath, and his soul plunged into the Fires of Hell to frizzle and fry throughout eternity.

Sunday newspapers were not considered religious, although my father went to the Devil to the extent of buying them each Sunday and permitting my brothers and myself to read the comic sections. Usually we went to Pelty's Book Store for them after church, bringing home the St. Louis *Globe-Democrat*, the *Republic* and the *Post-Dispatch*, together with a horde of small boys whose parents would not permit them to read anything on Sunday but the Bible, and who therefore came to our house and sprawled all over the place reading the comics and the magazine sections. My father was severely criticized for buying the Sunday newspapers, but he persisted in his wickedness. My prayerful uncle would not permit them in his house; indeed, all of his books but the Bibles remained in a locked case from Saturday night to Monday morning. But when my brothers and myself passed his home with the Sunday papers under our arms he always stopped us, and kept us waiting on the sidewalk for half an hour or more while he glanced at them and eagerly devoured the news. But he would not let us come in while we had the papers; he would meet us on the walk, and we were not old enough to object.

My father finally became very tired of this practice, and himself went after the papers. The first day he did this, my uncle was on his front porch, waiting for us to come by, and he stopped my father and reached for one of the papers. But my father would not let him have any of them.

"No, no," he said. "You do not believe in Sunday papers."

And thereafter my uncle did not read our Sunday papers, although he occasionally visited us in the afternoon and looked at them, after expressing his sorrow at finding them in our house. Once he found his son sprawled in our yard guffawing over the antics of the Yellow Kid when he should have been at a meeting of the Loyal Temperance Legion, lifting his childish voice against the Rum Demon. My uncle chased the lad home with threats of punishment, and then himself took up the funny section.

Baseball games were played by the ungodly on the outskirts of the town on Sunday, but the game was frowned upon by the Preachers and the Brothers and Sisters, who denounced it as a lure of Satan and predicted dire spiritual tortures for the players. Small boys who attended the games were soundly whipped, but occasionally we became so feverish with the desire to witness a contest that we slipped away from home and watched the game, pretending that we were going to visit relatives and listen to hymns played on an organ. But there were always spies of the Lord at the game to tell on us. It was this opposition to Sunday baseball that drove my younger brother out of the Methodist Sunday school, only a little while after I myself had abandoned the church. He was in the class taught by Brother Benjamin Marbury, a lawyer and an exceedingly loud and bitter antagonist of baseball. He denounced the game before his class one day, and my brother said that he could not see anything wrong with it. Brother Marbury stared at him sternly.

"Would Jesus Christ attend a baseball game on Sunday if He were here?" he demanded.

My brother said he did not know, but thought He would, and Brother Marbury immediately knelt and asked God to forgive the blasphemy. My brother was infuriated and never went back to Sunday school. His comment was: "What did he have to bring Jesus Christ into it for?"

2

WE arose at the usual hour on Sunday morning, perhaps a little later, and immediately after breakfast began to get ready for Sunday school. There was hair to comb, shoes to polish in the kitchen, cravats to tie around necks that had become enlarged and reddened by various activities on the playing fields, and there were nickels to secrete for the collection boxes. Worse, there were Sunday-school lessons and Golden Texts to learn, and the catechism to memorize. Dressed in our Sunday suits, our hair slicked moistly to our heads and Sunday-school pamphlets in our hands, my two brothers and I went solemnly down to Newman's corner, turned into the unnamed street that ran past Elmwood Seminary and then into Columbia Street and so to the Southern Methodist church.

Ordinarily a trip downtown was a great deal of fun; we tripped each other, poked each other in the ribs or had two or three fights *en route*, varying with the warmth of our friendship for other boys we met upon the way. But on Sunday we went solemnly and fearfully, first Emmett, then myself and then Fred, according to age and stature. We met other similar groups, arrayed as we were in their Sunday suits and clutching their lesson pamphlets, and our greetings were subdued and formal. We converged upon the church, and all over town the bells tolled and the faithful marched to hear God's intimates explain His written word, and tell us calmly and definitely what He meant by the most obscure passages in His Book.

We sat in church for an hour and a half listening to various versions of the Hebraic fairy tales. In our church the Sunday-school room was set apart from the main auditorium, but occasionally the attendance was so large that it overflowed into the church proper. To most of us Sunday school was torture, and I have no doubt that it is still torture to most children. It may be that I did not learn a great deal about the Bible in Sunday school, but I do know that it was in Sunday school that I first began to doubt the Book. I was naturally curious and inquisitive, and even then, young as I was, I could not swallow the miracles of Jonah and the whale, and the idea of the virgin birth of Jesus I considered absurd, because in common with most small-town boys I had a very definite knowledge of the procedure employed in bringing babies into the world. Up to the age of seven or eight I thought the doctor brought them in his suitcase, or that they grew on bushes in the backyard and were plucked when ripe, but after I began to loaf around the livery stable and the Post Office building I acquired more correct information. Nor could I believe that Noah's Ark would have held two of every living thing then upon the earth. But the Preachers and Brothers and Sisters insisted that these things were literally true; they denounced anyone who doubted and sought for symbolical meaning as an unbeliever and a blasphemous son of Satan.

My sister, at the age of ten, was the object of special prayers and solemn conferences because, for no other reason than that she wanted to be contrary, she expressed a doubt of the Virgin Birth. She was in Mrs. Judge Garter's Sunday-school class at the time, but she did not like Mrs. Carter and disagreed with her when she thought she could do so without subsequent punishment. Mrs. Carter frequently told her pupils, all little girls about eight or ten years old, of the marvelous manner in in which Christ came into the world, but she told it so vaguely that none of them had any real understanding of it. One Sunday morning, after Mrs. Carter had read something about the Virgin Birth, my sister said flatly that she did not believe it.

"Don't believe what?" asked Mrs. Carter.

"Virgin birth," said my sister. "I think it's foolish."

Unfortunately, she made this observation at a time when the whole Sunday school was quiet save for the mumbling of the catechism in various classes, and her thin little voice reached every corner of the room. And instantly there was a horrified silence, broken after a moment by someone who said: "It's that blasphemous little Asbury girl." Mrs. Carter was stunned; the effect upon her was the same as if God had walked in the door and announced that Buddha, or Zoroaster, and not Jesus Christ, was His son. She stared for a moment at this brash child who had defied religion and, in effect, denounced the Holy Book.

"Mary!" she said terribly. "Do you realize what you have done?"

My sister's conception of virgin birth, or of any sort of birth, was decidedly hazy. She thought Virgin Birth meant that Christ had been born in a stable, and she knew perfectly well that no nice child would be born in such a place. Anyhow, she had heard so much about it that she had become quite bored by it, and she felt it incumbent upon her to deny it. But from Mrs. Carter's attitude she knew that she had said a terrible thing; at first she thought of recanting, but she looked about and felt of herself, and when she did not see any avenging angels entering and could find no sign that she had been stricken, she stuck to her guns.

"Well," she said, "I just don't believe it."

"Mary!" said Mrs. Carter. "Go home and pray!"

So my sister went home, but I do not think that she prayed. Mrs. Carter and the Preacher called that afternoon and told my father and mother what had been said and done that day in God's house, and there was a considerable to-do about it, both Mrs. Carter and the Preacher dropping to their knees and praying, and insisting, that my sister pray also for forgiveness. But my father and mother took the attitude that since my sister did not know what she was talking about, she probably had not sinned to any great extent. But it was a good many years before she again had courage to express a doubt as to the Virgin Birth. And if she goes to Heaven she will probably find that Mrs. Carter and the Preacher have instructed St. Peter to catechize her about it, and not to admit her until she had atoned fully for her heinous offense at the age of ten.

3

SOME of our families in which there was an unfortunate excess of girls permitted them to have callers on Sunday afternoon, but such affairs were conducted in a prim and prissy manner. Holiness was the motif. The boy, if he had been a good lad all week and had done nothing to affront God or the Preacher, was dressed in his Sunday suit, and the young lady wore the frock that was kept in reserve for weddings, funerals, and baptizings, and those cannibalistic exercises called the Lord's Supper. And it was definitely understood that if a boy called on a girl on a Sunday, he was courting her, and intended to propose marriage. They could not talk; they must converse, and their conversation must be on subjects both inspiring and uplifting. These bons mots that are now known as wise cracks were frowned upon, and a repetition of them resulted in the young gentleman being shown the door.

The piano and the phonograph, in those houses which possessed such wonders, were under lock and key and covered over with draperies to hide them, for it was God's day and God wanted no foolishness. The girl's father sat in various strategic places about the house, moving from one to another as his suspicions of the boy's intentions arose and subsided, and her mother moved solemnly to and fro in her best crinkly silk dress. There was nothing of joy in the hearts of a boy and girl who underwent the torture of the Sunday-afternoon call; to paraphrase the immortal song of Casey, God had struck them out.

The first, and almost the last, young lady upon whom I called on a Sunday afternoon lived near the waterworks, and her father and mother, rocking solemnly upon the front porch and doubtless reflecting gloomily upon the wickedness of the race, presented such a forbidding spectacle that I walked four times around the block before venturing in. But at length I did, and the then idol of my heart greeted me at the front door. Ordinarily she would have seen me coming, and she would have poked her head out of the window and yelled: "Hey! I'll be out in a minute." Then we would have piled side by side into the lawn swing and begun swapping trade-lasts, and the air would have been thick with appreciative squeals and "he saids" and "she saids." But this was Sunday, a day given over to the glory that is religion, and so she met me at the door with a prim and pretty curtsy. Her father gave me a gentle but suspicious greeting, because to the religious parent every boy thinks of a girl only in terms of seduction, and her mother stopped her rocking chair long enough to inquire:

"Did you go to Sunday school to-day, Herbie?"

"Yes, ma'am."

"What was the Golden Text?" she demanded, suspiciously. I told her and she asked:

"Did you stay to church?"

"Yes, ma'am."

"Brother Jenkins preached such a beautiful sermon."

"Yes, ma'am."

And then she smiled a gentle smile, sighed a dolefully religious sigh and told her daughter that she could take me into the parlor, that holy of holies which was darkened and unused during the week, but opened on Sundays for callers and on other special occasions such as funerals and weddings. The room was extraordinarily gloomy, because the curtains were never raised enough to let in a great deal of light, and it smelled musty from being closed all week. And invariably the gloom was added to by a crayon portrait of the head of the house, a goggle-eyed enlargement of a very ordinary photograph by Trappe, which stood on an easel in a corner.

I had considered this call an occasion, and with the aid of my elder sister who was visiting us from Memphis, I had made an elaborate toilet and had been permitted to wear my Sunday suit. But I did not have a good time; I had known this girl a long time and admired her intensely, but she seemed suddenly to have changed. She sat stiffly on one side of the room near a window, hands folded demurely in her lap, and

I sat as stiffly on the other. We inquired coldly concerning each other's health, and I had prepared in my mind a suitable and, indeed, quite holy comment on certain aspects of our school life and was about to deliver it when her mother called gently from the porch:

"Don't play the piano, dear: it's Sunday."

My observation went unuttered, and we sat for some little time in an embarrassed silence broken only by the crunch of her mother's rocking chair and the crooning melody of a hymn, each wishing to Heaven that the other was elsewhere. I yearned to hear the piano, but this instrument, with its delightful tinkle and its capacity for producing ragtime, was generally regarded as a hellish contraption; in fact, any sort of fast music was considered more or less sinful. If there had been an organ in the house, the young lady would have been permitted to play it, and we could have sung from the family hymn book, provided we did so in proper humility. But there was only a piano, and it was taboo. Presently the mother spoke again:

"Don't play the phonograph, dear; it's Sunday."

This admonition was modified later by permission to play an organ record of the hymn, "Face to Face," and we played it over five times before the mother got tired of hearing it. She said, "You'd better stop now, dear; it's Sunday." Then she suggested that we turn to other means of entertainment.

"Perhaps Herbie would like to look at the album, dear. Would you, Herbie?"

"Yes, ma'am," I said.

So we looked at the album, stiffly and in silence, the sacred book held on our knees, but we were very careful that our knees did not touch. We dared not giggle at the sight of the bushy-whiskered members of the young lady's family, and made no comment on their raiment, which we rightly considered outlandish. We turned the pages and stared, and the girl explained.

"That's Uncle Martin."

"Taken when he went to Niagara Falls on his honeymoon, dear," said her mother. "Uncle Martin was a great traveler."

"Yes, ma'am," I said, feeling that comment was expected.

"Wouldn't you like to travel, Herbie?"

"Yes, ma'am."

"Well, be a good boy and read your Bible and maybe some day God will make you a great traveler."

"Yes, ma'am."

"But don't travel on Sunday, Herbie."

"No, ma'am."

And crunch went the rocker and we turned another page, to find Aunt Ella smiling gently at us through a mass of glorious flounces and trains and switches. We learned from the mother that Aunt Ella had been converted, at an extraordinarily early age, during a revival near Hazel Run, and had lived a singularly devout and godly life. Then we looked through the stereopticon at various places of interest, murmuring our awe when the mother swished gently into the room and pointed out, in a view of Niagara Falls, the exact spot where Uncle Martin had stood. It was, she explained, one of God's rocks.

To my knowledge this family had some very comical stereopticon views, scenes depicting the life of an unfortunate tramp who was kicked heartily and effectively at every place he applied for nourishment, but we did not see them on Sunday afternoon. They were Saturday-night stuff. Saturday night was nigger night in Farmington, and the whole town let down the bars somewhat. That was the night when those who drank got tight, and when those who bathed got wet, and when those who had amorous intentions did their best to carry them out. Had I called on Saturday night I should have been permitted to enjoy the adventures of the unfortunate tramp, but not on Sunday. They had been put away, under lock and key in the writing desk, and would not be brought out until Monday. They were not calculated to promulgate a proper respect for the Lord's Day; they were considered downright wicked one day a week and funny the other six.

Even in my infatuated condition an hour or so of this was quite enough. Ordinarily this girl and I had much in common; at that time I ranked her high among the beautiful flowers of God, and had I stopped at her house on a week day we would have had gleeful and uproarious converse, although even then we would have been liable to religious instruction and catechism from every snooping Brother and Sister who saw us. But the taboos that this Christian family had raised on its holy day stood between us and could not be broken down; we were horribly uncomfortable in each other's presence, and we never got over it. She was never afterward the same girl. And when I took myself and my Sunday suit into the sunlight of the porch her mother stopped rocking and crooning hymns long enough to demand.

"Are you going to church to-night, Herbie?"

"Yes, ma'am," I replied. "I got to."

And so I went out of the gate and away from there. This sort of thing in the homes of Farmington drove all of the boys to more or less open revolt as rapidly as they reached an age at which they felt able to defy parental and churchly authority. By the time I left the town the Sunday-afternoon callers, except those who made unavoidable duty calls, were to be found only in the homes of the ungodly, where there was music and pleasure and gayety, where the parlor was wide open seven days a week and the phonograph blared and the piano tinkled whenever anyone wanted to hear them. To these houses also went the girls from the devout families for clandestine meetings with their sweethearts; they could not entertain anyone in the dismal mausoleums into which their fathers and mothers had transformed their homes. Many a small-town romance has been blighted by the Sunday-afternoon call.

CHAPTER IV

AGENTS OF GOD

1

IN FARMINGTON we had not only those Preachers who had
had been ordained to the ministry and so licensed to preach
by both God and man, but the town was overrun with volunteers, Brothers and Sisters who shouted the word of God
whenever they could find an audience, who gave the testimony
at the camp meetings, the protracted meetings, and at those
orgies conducted by the professional evangelist who chased
the Devil from any town that would guarantee him a fat fee.
These Preachers and their allies controlled Farmington to a
very large extent, and when they were defeated, at elections or

otherwise, they raised their voices in howls of denunciation and called upon God to punish the guilty. It was many years before I learned that a candidate endorsed by a Preacher was not necessarily called by God to assume the office.

It was essential for any man who wanted to hold public office to profess religion and be seen at church, and usually the more noise he made in religious gatherings, the greater his chances of success at the polls. If any candidate dared to hold views contrary to those of the godly, a vile whispering campaign was started against him, and his personal life was raked over and bared with many gloating references to the Christian duty of the people to punish this upstart. Occasionally the ungodly or anti-religious element elected a mayor or what not, but generally religion triumphed and thanks were offered to God, and then throughout his term the office-holder was harassed by pious hypocrites seeking favors and special privilege. My father, as county surveyor and city clerk, was constantly being checked up on to determine if he remained steadfast in the faith.

I do not think that my father was regarded as a first-class Christian in Farmington; I am sure that in many quarters it was felt that he was more or less disgracing his ancestry because he did not bound to his feet at camp meetings and similar gatherings and make a holy show of himself with hypocritical testimony. He went to church, and until I was old enough to do pretty much as I pleased, he saw to it that I went also, and to Sunday school and Epworth League and other places where the Methodist God could take a peek at my soul. But he was only passively religious; he showed no tremendous enthusiasm for the Wesleyan Deity, and he never made a particularly active effort to keep me in the path that, according to some, leads to spiritual glory.

In a religious sense I was annoyed much less by my father and my mother than I was by the busybodies who seemed to be appointed by the Lord to take care of everybody's business but their own. Most of the religious instruction that I received came from volunteers, either relatives of my parents, or Brothers and Sisters whom I encountered during my pathetic efforts to have a good time. And, of course, from the Preacher. To many of these I put questions; I asked them to explain certain things in the Bible and in the church service that I did not understand, and which seemed to conflict with the little definite knowledge that I had of life and human beings. Invariably I was told that the Bible needed no explaining; I was merely to believe it and have faith.

I was afraid of the Preachers in Farmington, and of the Brothers and Sisters, desperately afraid of them, because they filled my mind with horrible pictures of Hell and the roaring fires of old Nick; their object in talking religion to small boys seemed to be to frighten them into being good. And I think that most of the other boys were afraid of them, too, except such brave souls as my cousin, Barney Blue, who was a "bad boy" and afraid of neither God nor Devil. One of my great moments was when I heard Barney tell a prying old Brother to go to hell. And curiously enough, and incomprehensibly to many of the good old people of Farmington, Barney is to-day exceedingly prosperous and well thought of in his community.

But there were very few like Barney; most of us trembled in our boots, even the red-topped ones we were so proud of, when a Preacher or a Brother or Sister came snooping about, head bowed under its burden of religious horror, and demanded information as to our conduct and the condition of our souls. In the cities the cry of the youngsters was

"Cheese it, the cop," but in Farmington it was "Look out, there's a Preacher!" We could not start a game of marbles anywhere in town but one of them, or else a Brother or Sister, did not pounce upon us and demand to know if we were playing "for keeps." And since we invariably were, and did not know enough to tell the Preacher what was politely called a fib, the game stopped then and there while we absorbed a little religion and learned that God abhorred little boys who played for keeps.

We were told that God had His eye on us when we did such things, and that our Guardian Angels put black marks in their little books every time we shot a marble.

"You must give your heart to Jesus," we were told. "He will not let you dwell in the Heavenly Mansions if you persist in this sinful practice."

We used to play marbles in a vacant lot behind the Christian church, and it was a very fine playground, with a level stretch on which the marbles rolled beautifully. But we had to give it up, because the lot was near the home of a Sister, who spent most of her waking hours in front of her window, staring out through the curtains in a constant search for sin and scandal. We had no more than drawn the ring and legged for first shot than she came out on her porch and shouted:

"Are you boys playing for keeps?"

And we answered in unison, politely, as we had been taught:

"Yes, ma'am."

She stopped the game, swooping down upon us with the glint of the Heaven-born fanatic in her eye. She told us that we were wicked and sinful and blasphemous and Heaven knows what else besides to play for keeps in the very shadow of a House of God. She invariably threatened us with punishment ranging from spanking to everlasting torment in Hell, and if we dared to say anything to her other than the conventional "Yes, ma'am," she said we were saucy and threatened to telephone our mothers. Occasionally she did so, and a marble game behind the Christian church was then followed by the wails of little boys being led into the woodshed. She performed her war dance many times, and finally we went to play near the livery stable. The atmosphere there was not so uplifting, but at least we were in peace, for the hostlers had no interest at all in our immortal souls, although they were very much interested in who won the marbles.

2

THE livery stables in Farmington were a sort of symbol of the heretical element of the town. The big Mayberry & Byington barn, down the block from Braun's Hotel and Saloon, was a particularly delightful place to loaf; it was infested by sinners, abandoned wretches who swore horrible oaths, smoked cigarettes, and drank whisky and gin out of big bottles. The politicians loafed there at such times as they felt they would not be seen by the more godly part of our citizenry.

Two of our most celebrated darkies, Uncle Louis Burks and Uncle Mose Bridges, spent most of their time at the Mayberry barn, and we considered them quite fascinating, especially Uncle Louis. He regaled us with tales of the days when, in the South before the Civil War, he had no duties except be the father of as many children as possible; that was his job. He estimated the number of his progeny anywhere from fifty to five hundred, according to the amount of liquor he had consumed before counting, and we generally gave him the benefit of the doubt and called it five hundred. We ranked him with the great fathers of the Bible, and I recall that it seemed to me somewhat strange that the preachers did not offer Uncle Louis's achievements as proof of the truth of certain portions of the Book.

Uncle Mose's principal claim to our attention was his dog, a sad-eyed little mongrel that trotted at the end of a string everywhere Uncle Mose went. We were permitted to play with the dog occasionally, much to the disgust of our parents, as we invariably went home scratching. Both Uncle Louis and Uncle Mose were regarded as sinners, partly on account of their color. It was not believed that a black man could enter the Kingdom of Heaven, although the deluded creatures had churches and prayed to God. And then their domestic arrangements were somewhat haphazard, and Uncle Louis frequently boasted that he did not marry all the mothers of his children before the War. Both he and Uncle Mose were familiar figures around Farmington for many years; they did odd jobs at the homes of the godly, and for their pay received part cash and part religious lectures and prayers. They thrived on the cash, and apparently the prayers did not hurt them.

It was at the livery stable, also, that the drummers from St. Louis, waiting for rigs to take them to the towns of the lead-mining district around Bonne Terre, Flat River and Elvins, left their stocks of stories. The coming of a drummer was an event with us; it meant that we should hear things that were not meant for our little ears, and that for a little while at least we could revel in the sight of a man given over to sin and seemingly enjoying it. He used to assure us solemnly that playing marbles for keeps was not a sin anywhere in the world

but in Farmington, and tell stories, which we regarded as fan-
ciful untruths, of towns in which little boys did not have to
go to Sunday school.

The drummer came in on the herdic from De Lassus
before the interurban railroad was built, and he was generally
a gorgeous spectacle. He was not welcomed in our best
homes, and even his presence in church was not considered
a good omen for the forces of righteousness, so he could usually be found loafing in front of the livery stable or dozing in
a chair tilted against the wall of the St. Francis Hotel. He
brought with him not only the latest stories, but the most
advanced raiment; the first peg-top trousers ever seen in
Farmington adorned the legs of a shoe drummer traveling
out of St. Louis, and they created a furor and established a
style. Soon our most stylish dressers had them.

Besides being the abode of wickedness and the lair of
Satan, and therefore an extraordinarily fascinating place, the
livery stable was also the principal loafing place of a darky
who had fits. He was one of our town characters, and was
regarded by myself and the other boys as a person of remarkable accomplishments. We felt that to be able to have fits set
him above us; we gloated enormously when he suddenly
shrieked, fell to the ground and began foaming at the mouth.
Our attitude toward him was respectful, and he appreciated
it. He was, it seemed to me, proud of his fits. I have known
him to rise, finally, brush himself off and ask, simply:

"Was it a good one?"

Generally we thought it was. This darky became such an
attraction for us that for a long time, when a group of us
could find nothing interesting to do, and when there was for
the moment no one in sight to remind us of our duty to God
and the church, it was the custom for one of us to say:

"Let's go over to the livery stable and see Tod have a fit."

We thereupon trooped solemnly to the big barn and gathered in a circle about the darky, who was generally sitting against the side of the building whittling on a stick. We watched him silently for a while, and then someone mustered up courage enough to say:

"Going to have a fit to-day, Tod?"

With the instinct of the true artist, Tod ignored us for a time, intent upon his whittling. Finally he gave us brief attention.

"Maybe," he said, and returned to his task.

And then suddenly he uttered a blood-curdling shriek and tumbled headlong from his chair. We watched, fascinated, uttering little murmurs of "ah!" as he writhed and moaned, and when it was all over we settled back with a little sigh of satisfaction. We felt that we had seen a first-rate performance, and when the darky had a fit in front of the Post Office, or in the yard of the courthouse, his audience was increased by as many boys and men as were downtown, shopkeepers leaving their wares to run across and watch.

There was nothing of callousness in our attitude toward the darky. My own feeling in the matter was that Tod was having fits for our benefit, and because he enjoyed it, but at length I came to learn that he could not help it, that the poor fellow was ill. Then I was sorry for him, and one day I asked one of our most prominent Brothers why Tod had fits. He immediately seized upon the question to give me some religious instruction.

"He has sinned," said the Brother, "and God is punishing him."

He elaborated his statement, explaining that Tod had probably neglected to attend Sunday school, or had not read his Bible, and that he had thus become a blasphemous sinner and was being properly dealt with. He pointed out that I, too, might grow up and have fits if I was not a good boy. Now, I did not want to have fits, and neither did I want to be a good boy. I wanted to have some fun; I wanted to run about, and play marbles, and go swimming, and put tick-tacks against people's window on Halloween night. I wanted to do all sorts of things that good boys did not do, yet I most certainly did not want to have fits.

"But, Uncle Si," I said, "how do you know that God is making him have fits? And why does God do it?"

"Herbie!" He was shocked. "You are blasphemous! You must not question the wisdom of the Almighty. I have faith, and I believe in God and the holiness of His acts. I know that this man must have sinned, or God would not punish him so."

I was not prepared to confound this faulty logic; it was not then the business of small boys to question anything their elders told them, but to accept without comment the pearls of wisdom that fell from bewhiskered lips. But it seemed to me small business for God to be engaged upon. Yet it did not cause me great surprise, for I had long known that the God who pressed so heavily upon Farmington was a conception of unutterable cruelty, an omnipotent Being whose greatest joy lay in singling out the weak and lowly and inflicting horrible tortures upon them, to the vast and gloating satisfaction of the Brothers and their kind.

Some time afterward, because I was worried over this torturing and punishment of the darky whose writhings had now become less an amusing exhibit than a terrible manifestation of the Almighty, I asked another Brother how he knew that God had a hand in it. But neither he nor Uncle Si ever told me. None of them were ever able to tell me how they knew so well what God wanted and what God did not want; they merely left with me the impression that on occasion they walked with God and that God spoke to them and asked their advice on the conduct of the human race. But the source of their information I could not determine.

I have never found anyone who could satisfy my curiosity on this point; I never then, or later, found a religious enthusiast who would admit that he was offering merely his personal interpretation of the utterances that other men had credited to the Almighty. But there was nothing that entered the mind of God that the Preachers and the Brothers and Sisters of Farmington did not know and that they could not explain and apply to local affairs. They knew precisely what was a sin and what was not, and it was curious that the sins were invariably things from which they received no pleasure. Nor was anything which paid a profit a sin. They knew very well that God considered it a sin to play cards or dance, but that He thought it only good business practice to raise the price of beans or swindle a fellow citizen in the matter of town lots, or refuse credit to the poor and suffering.

3

AS I grew older, and began to be skeptical of what I was told, I became increasingly annoyed not only by the mental mannerisms of these people, but by their physical mannerisms as well. Not only did they walk as if their soles were greased, sliding and slipping about, but they talked as if their tongues were greased also. Their language was oily; they poured out their words unctuously, with much roundabout phrasing and unnecessary language. If they wanted to tell about a man going across the street from the Court House to the Post Office they would take him up the hill past the Masonic cemetery, with side trips to Jerusalem and other Jewish centers. If I went downtown and met a man like Sheriff Rariden, who will always have a place in my affections because he permitted his son Linn and myself to roam the jail yard and stare through the bars at the nigger prisoners, he would say:

"How're you, Herbie? How're your folks?"

But if I met a Preacher the greeting was this: "Good afternoon, Herbert. And how are your dear father and mother?"

And then he patted me on the head, pinched my arm, and padded away, sliding greasily along the pavement, his eagle eye alert for little boys playing marbles or for other signs of sin. He might have been skinny and pitifully in need of food, but nevertheless I thought of him as greasy. He had about him an unwholesome atmosphere; I could not be comfortable in his presence. I felt that he had to be watched, and when I became old enough to understand some of the looks that he bestowed upon the young and feminine members of his flock I realized that he should have been.

I had not lived very many years before I learned to look upon Preachers, and their familiars, the Brothers and Sisters, as useless incumbrances upon an otherwise fair enough earth. But while I hated all of them, with a few natural exceptions, the one I always hated most was the current pastor of our Southern Methodist church. He was my spiritual father, the guardian of my soul and the director of my life in the hereafter, and he tried to see to it that I went into the hereafter with proper respect for him and a proper respect for his God. I had to call him Brother and be very meek and gentle in his presence, and stand without moving while he patted me on the head, asked me fool questions, and told me how much God loved little boys and girls. He called me a "manly little fellow," which annoyed me exceedingly, and I have the word of my young nephew that small boys are still annoyed by it.

But he made it quite clear, out of his profound knowledge of the wishes of the Almighty, that God did not want little boys and girls to have a good time. Quite the contrary. God wanted them to do exactly what the Preacher told them to do; He wanted them to accept the Preacher as their guide and their philosopher and believe everything they were told, without fretting him with unanswerable and therefore blasphemous questions. He wanted the little boys and girls to spend most of their time praying to Him to "gimme this and gimme that," and the rest of it being little gentlemen and little ladies, solemn and subdued, speaking only when spoken to and answering promptly when called. God told the Preacher, who relayed the message on to me very impressively, that it was a sin to play marbles on Sunday, or to play for keeps at any time; that it was a sin to roll hoops on the sidewalk in front of the church or rattle a stick against the picket fence in front of the parsonage. Everything that I wanted to do, everything that seemed to hold any promise of fun or excitement, was a sin.

But it was not a sin to saw wood for the Preacher, or to carry huge armfuls of sticks and fill his kitchen bin, and it was not a sin to mow his lawn or rake the trash in his back yard. The children of the godly were permitted to do these things because of the profound love which the Preacher bore for them; his motto was "Suffer little children to come unto me, and I will put them to work." And since by his own admission the Preacher was a Man of God, we were permitted to perform these labors for nothing. A boy was paid twenty-five to fifty cents, enormous and gratifying sums in those days, if he mowed the lawn or raked the trash for a family given over to sin, but if he did the job for a Preacher or a devout Brother, he received nothing but a pat on the back and a prayer, or he could listen to a verse from the Bible and a lecture on his duty to serve the Lord and, incidentally, the self-appointed ambassadors of the Lord.

Once when I was about twelve years old our pastor telephoned my mother and asked that I be sent to his house to help him perform certain tasks which should have been done by the darky men of all work about town. But our family did not wish to offend the Preacher, so I did the work. And it was hard work. I toiled all morning cleaning out the Preacher's woodshed and stacking split stove wood in neat piles, and then I carried in enough to fill two big wooden boxes in the kitchen. During this time the Preacher sat in his study, holding communion with God, and I presume, reading the Scriptures. Occasionally he came out to the woodshed to superintend my work, ordering me to do this and do that and scolding me because I did not work faster, but he did none of the work himself. And when I was through he told me to come into his study and receive payment. I hurried after him, very weary, but with pleasant visions of a quarter floating before my eyes. I believed that was the least I should receive, and to me it was a great deal of money; properly expended at McKinney's or Otto Rottger's, it would keep me in jawbreakers for more than a week, and there might be enough left to buy a bag of peewees or an agate.

But I did not receive the twenty-five cents. The Preacher closed the door when we got into his study, and then he commanded me to kneel. He put a hand on my shoulder, and he said:

"My dear boy, I am going to pray for you. I am going to ask the Lord Jesus to enter your heart and make you a good boy."

And then he knelt and prayed somewhat in this fashion: "O Lord Jesus, bless this little boy who has this day performed labor in Thy behalf," etc.

It was all very confusing. I went home somewhat in doubt as to whether the Preacher or God owned the woodshed.

But labor of little boys was not all that the Preachers got for nothing. They were inveterate beggars, and all of them had fine, highly developed noses for chickens and other dainties; it was seldom that a family could have a chicken or turkey dinner without the Preacher dropping in. It is true that their salaries were not large, but they had free use of the parsonage, and they were not in dire circumstances at all. Yet they always had their hands out, grasping; they were ecclesiastical tramps begging for a donation. In our town we used to give showers for them; many families made periodical donations to the Pastor, and sometimes there were surprise parties, when the Preacher and his wife were led into a room and shown piles of old clothing, food and discarded furniture, all of which was sent next day to the parsonage. The Preacher was always pathetically grateful for these things; he would kneel in the midst of them and offer a prayer for the souls of the good people who had thus given him the clutterings of their cellars and attics, which they had no further use for. He seldom had enough self-respect to refuse them.

4

THE notion was prevalent in Farmington, among the Brothers and Sisters, that the Preachers were their servants and should peddle God to them 365 days a year. It was felt also that their wives should be constantly at the Lord's work; that they should be at home at all times, available for consultation and prayer meetings, and that when they went abroad they should dress soberly and walk with due humility. The wife of Brother Court, one of our Methodist pastors, was severely criticized for her departure from this formula of conduct. Apparently the Courts had means other than the salary paid them by the church, and they kept a maid, which in itself was enough to arouse suspicion that Mrs. Court was not a true servant of the Lord.

But the straw that broke the religious back of the Courts and hastened the end of Brother Court's ministry was the fact that Mrs. Court took a nap each afternoon. This was considered nothing less than scandalous, and for a long time our Brothers and Sisters refused to believe that the wife of a man of God should so far forget herself as to lie abed when she might be praying or sitting at her front window looking through the curtains for a sin to happen. But the story persisted, and was broadcast by a discharged servant who swore that with her own eyes she had seen Mrs. Court sound asleep at three o'clock in the afternoon. Finally two Sisters appointed themselves a committee of investigation. They rang the bell at the parsonage one afternoon, and told the maid that they had called to join Mrs. Court in afternoon prayer, and, although they did not say it, backbiting gossip.

"Mrs. Court," said the maid, "is asleep and cannot be disturbed. Can you call later?"

They could not. They had barely strength enough to get home, but after prayer they revived sufficiently to sally forth and carry the awful news throughout the town. There could no longer be any doubt. The wife of the Pastor of the Southern Methodist church took a nap in the afternoon. The Sisters had called, and had been so informed by the maid, and while a few chronic doubters remained, the vast majority realized that in a matter involving such serious consequences to Mrs. Court's spiritual welfare, a matter that directly affected and almost destroyed her chances of going to Heaven, the Sisters could not tell a lie.

So Brother Court soon resigned and accepted a call to a town where members of his family could sleep when they felt like it, and could even snore without jeopardizing their immortal souls. Nor did his successor last very long. He was an Englishman, and spoke in a high nasal voice, pronouncing his words, very distinctly, syllable by syllable. He was criticized for several reasons. One was that his favorite phrase was "and an-gels can do no more," and it was felt that it was somewhat blasphemous to mention angels so often before mixed company. And then he spoke from notes, whereas it was a custom of our Pastors to preach solely out of divine inspiration at the moment of delivery.

There was much talk about the new Preacher's notes, and it was felt that, somehow, he was lacking in devotion to God; many Brothers and Sisters argued that if he were really a Man of God he would not have to use notes, but would be inspired and filled with words as he rose in the pulpit. His finish came the Sunday morning that the wind blew through an opened window and scattered his notes, so that he had to leave the pulpit and chase the scraps up and down the aisle before he could proceed with his discourse. This was regarded as direct evidence that God had deserted him, and he left town soon afterward.

5

THE personalities of the preachers of my home town, impressed as they were upon my growing, plastic mind, probably will remain with me always, but I am thankful that for the most part their names elude me. I remember clearly, however, Brother Jenkins and Brother Fontaine, of our Southern Methodist church; Brother Nations, of the so-called Christian church; Brother Hickok, of the Presbyterian church, and, clearest of all, Brother Lincoln McConnell, the professional itinerant evangelist who "converted" me with the aid of half a dozen strong-armed and strong-lunged Brothers and Sisters who dragged and pushed me down the aisle of the church to the mourners' bench, where I was surrounded and overwhelmed by "workers for the Lord."

Brother Jenkins I recall as a meek, thin little man with a sad smile and a classical appetite for fried chicken. At the time I was very much in awe of him, and listened to his every utterance with the most profound respect. I thought him saintly, and concluded that he and God were the closest sort of friends, and that the Deity would not dare launch upon a plan for a new universe or start a new; war without consulting Brother Jenkins. But in truth he was probably only undernourished. Brother Jenkins was a demon quoter of platitudes and Biblical passages; nothing happened that it did not remind him of a quotation from the Bible.

Brother Fontaine was a plump man who would have been jovial and possibly likable—that is giving him the benefit of a great doubt—if he had not been so burdened by the troubles of God and if he had not been so frightfully aware of the responsibilities of his position as a recipient and promulgator of Heavenly wisdom and commands. He officiated at the wedding of my sister, principally because our family belonged to his church and the presence of another preacher at the wedding would have deprived Brother Fontaine of a goodly fee and made an enemy of him for life. Christian charity does not function well when it hits the pocketbook. I think my sister would have preferred Brother Hickok, but she yielded to public opinion and Brother Fontaine got the job. He arrived at the house chewing tobacco, a habit of his which he disliked intensely in other men, but for which he found justification for himself in the belief that he walked with the Lord and that it was tacitly understood he was to have a little leeway.

He was excessively sanctimonious; and so was his wife. We have never forgiven her for her attitude at the wedding. I recall that she looked suspiciously from time to time at the groom, and watched the whole proceeding with an air that said there must of a necessity be something wrong somewhere; for one thing, there was quite a deal of laughter in our house that day, and that in itself was a sign that the Lord was not hovering over the housetop. Immediately after the ceremony Sister Fontaine paraded up front and began waving her hands back and forth before my sister's face, shouting at the top of her lungs: "Praise the Lord, Sister! Praise the Lord!" We gathered that she thought my sister should immediately fall upon her knees and thank God that she had at last acquired a husband, even though Sister Fontaine did not seem to think much of him. But we were greatly offended; we considered it a reflection on our family and wholly uncalled for, because my sister was, in fact, neither old nor homely, and she had had and rejected a great many first-class matrimonial opportunities.

I had an intense dislike for Brother Fontaine and his ways, and time has not softened my impression of him. He dearly loved to be the only man in a feminine gathering, where he could make heavy inroads upon the cake and ice cream and lay down the law to the adoring Sisters. I have seldom known a Preacher who was not afflicted with this mania, but in Brother Fontaine it had developed into a highly acute disease. I remember that he was always present at our house when the members of the Ladies' Aid Society came once each week for their bit of sewing for the heathen and to enjoy their pleasant afternoon of scandal. He had no business there; he did not sew and he did not contribute much to the symposium, but he listened avidly and ate heartily.

It was "Don't you think so, Brother Fontaine?" and "I fear I must take issue with you, Sister. The Lord provideth answers for all problems affecting human conduct." Fool talk like that.

It was the practice of our Southern Methodist preachers to stand at the door of the church after every performance and shake hands with the customers, making such remarks as "Praise the Lord, Sister! Get right with Jesus, Brother!" I always dreaded this part of the service, and several young girls told me that they did also. All of the preachers who did this, and almost all of them did, shook hands with a clammy pressure that put me in mind of an oyster, and it always seemed to me that when a lady customer passed through the door the Man of God invariably found it necessary to sigh.

But although I cannot rate Brother Fontaine very highly among the servants of the Lord, my younger brother consigned him to even lower depths. They went fishing together once, at Brother Fontaine's request, and Fred appeared at the parsonage with lunch, fishing tackle and car fare. Brother

Fontaine knelt and asked divine guidance for the expedition, and then they boarded a trolley car and went to De Lassus, to fish the St. Francis River around Blumeyer's Ford. Fred paid his fare.

"You must pay my fare, too, Fred," said Brother Fontaine. "I am the minister."

So Fred paid. There was nothing else that he could do; he was afraid that if he did not Brother Fontaine would whistle to God to call down an avenging angel armed with thunderbolts and lightning. Then it developed that Brother Fontaine had brought neither lunch nor fishing tackle; he had brought only himself, and being a Man of God that was sufficient. Perhaps he felt that since his influence with the Almighty was undoubtedly great enough to make the trip successful, Fred had no right to expect him to bear any of the expenses or furnish any equipment. So he used Fred's tackle and ate Fred's lunch, and when that was not enough for him he sent Fred a mile and a half to a farmhouse to buy a bottle of milk, for which Fred paid and which the reverend one guzzled without offering to share it.

Throughout the whole day Brother Fontaine alternately prayed and fished, but there must have been something wrong with his connecting line to Heaven, for he caught no fish. He finally turned the tackle over to Fred, with the remark that Fred had not brought the right sort of worms, and with the further explanation that worms being God's creatures as well as fish, God probably did not want the fish to eat them. Fred fished earnestly; he was ordinarily a good and successful fisherman, and it was a matter of pride with him not to go home without a string. But neither did Fred catch any fish, and he became increasingly annoyed at Brother Fontaine.

The preacher apparently labored under the delusion that Fred required religious instruction. He told, several times, the story of the loaves and the fishes, and many other Biblical fairy tales as well. Once, when Fred was anxiously watching his cork and felt certain that a perch was nibbling at his hook, Brother Fontaine stopped him to read the Sermon on the Mount from a Bible which he drew from his pocket. Everything he saw reminded him of something in the Scriptures. So passed the day, and when Fred came home that night, with no fish, he ate heavily of supper and then dared parental wrath by saying:

"No more of these damned preachers for me."

Brother Nations is probably Farmington's most illustrious gift to religion. It is true that he eventually resigned from the ministry and became Probate Judge and Principal of the High School, but he remained a steadfast adherent of the Protestant God and a singularly devout and godly man. I presume he still is, as he is the same Gilbert O. Nations who in 1924 ran for President as the candidate of what he called the American party, asking for the votes of the electorate on a pro-Ku Klux Klan and anti-everything else platform. I am told that he is now the editor of a magazine devoted to baiting the Catholics.

Once when Brother Nations was principal of the Farmington High School he whaled me because Barney Blue and I had thrown snowballs at Jake Schaeffer, the town truckman. I felt that the licking was coming to me and I bore no malice; only the week before I had thrown lumps of coal at Pete Anderson's house across the street and had been warned that the hurling of anything at all would result in punishment. But after the thrashing was over, Brother Nations told me that throwing snowballs at Jake Schaeffer was a sin against

God: that Christ had reference to it when he said: "Let him who is without sin cast the first stone." I could not plead that I was without sin, because it had been impressed on me by every Brother and Sister and Preacher that I met that I was practically broken out with it. But young and gullible as I was, Brother Nations' statement sounded silly.

I could understand that from Jake Schaeffer's viewpoint I had sinned, and grievously, because Jake was stooping over when the snowball struck and I had put a stone in the center of it to make the snow pack tighter; I was willing to admit that and repent. But what did God care if two boys smacked snowballs against a soft part of Jake's person? It seemed to me that if God had been really interested in the matter He would have advised Jake Schaeffer not to stoop over when two boys were abroad with snowballs. Thus He might have prevented a sin. Further, if God was as intelligent as I had been led to believe, He must have known that boys cannot resist the temptation to throw snowballs, and since He made both the boys and the snowballs He was responsible for the sin committed against Himself. But Brother Nations appeared to believe that God had permitted me to sin in order that I might taste the joys of castigatory rebuke. And I did.

Brother Hickok was the only Preacher of those days to whom I gave the slightest measure of respect. I had a genuine admiration for him, but it was not because he was a Preacher or because he pretended to any inside knowledge of the customs of Heaven or the thoughts and wishes of God. On the contrary, I have heard him admit that there were things in the Bible he did not understand, and I have heard him admit that there were passages in it that he did not particularly care for. But I liked him simply because he chewed tobacco without any effort at concealment, and played lawn tennis on the courts near our home, and because I suspected, every time I saw him wallop a tennis ball or bite a chunk from a slab of plug-cut, that he was Wild Bill Hickok in disguise.

About the time Brother Hickok came to Farmington I acquired a book devoted to the adventures of Wild Bill, Kit Carson, Buffalo Bill and other heroes of the Western plains, and of them all I liked Wild Bill best. He seemed to me to be everything that a man ought to be. He had more notches on his gun than any of the others, and it appeared that he could not so much as sneeze without a redskin biting the dust. I put the question of identity to Brother Hickok rather bluntly, and told him I would respect his confidence, but he denied it, although I gathered the impression that he was a relative of Wild Bill and, of course, mighty proud of him. But I was not satisfied, and for a long time I shadowed him in the manner set forth by Old and Young King Brady in that sterling nickel novel, "Secret Service," hoping to learn his secret. However, I never did solve the question to my own satisfaction.

But principally I admired Brother Hickok because he was the only Preacher I knew who did not proclaim incessantly that he was a Man of God and therefore entitled to the largest piece of pie, and because he was the only one who did not seem to be impressed by my relationship with Bishop Asbury. He didn't seem to give a damn about the Bishop; his only ambition, so far as I was concerned, was to beat me at tennis, which he did. But from the others, and from the Brothers and Sisters, I got the impression that the right reverend deceased, seated at God's right hand between Jesus Christ and St. Peter, perhaps crowding the latter a bit, had nothing to do but receive messages from the Almighty touching on my conduct, and relay them to me by whatever Preacher I happened to meet. For many years I thought that God and the Bishop had a consultation on my case every night.

I do not think that I shall ever forget Brother Lincoln McConnell, although I probably should not recognize him if I saw him to-day. I hope not. But for some eighteen long years I have cherished a compelling desire to stand him in a corner, minus his band and singers and his other aids to emotion, and then bind and gag him. After that I want to talk to him for hours and hours, embellishing my remarks with such florid words as I have acquired in various military and journalistic enterprises, and possibly inventing new ones for the occasion. He was responsible for the most miserable period of my life. But it was he, too, who definitely kept me from being a Preacher, or even a Brother, and so, perhaps, I should thank him. If he had let me alone I might at this moment be calling some other preacher Brother; I might be an intimate of God, and a walking Baedeker of Heaven; I might even be gloating over the glories of a Heaven paved with gold and populated by angels, all female, all beautiful, all amiable. Certainly I should not be given over to a life of sin; that is to say, I should not be having a pretty good time with this business of living.

Brother McConnell, as I write, is a pastor of a Baptist church in Oklahoma City, Okla., with occasional forays onto the Chautauqua platform, and is a potent force in the life of that abode of righteousness. But if reports are to be believed, there are even there those who consider him a blight. He has been the central figure in several rows that have undoubtedly redounded to the greater glory of God; he tried to prevent the citizens of his town from seeing one of the best American plays of recent years because it dealt a bit too truthfully with certain aspects of religious fanaticism, and he erected a radio broadcasting station which blanketed the city and forced the population to listen, willy-nilly, to his sermons and his ponderous pronouncements against sin.

I once wrote a magazine article in which I discussed a few of the activities of Brother McConnell, and he put me in my place in an interview which, it seems to me, shows that he has not changed a great deal since the time that I first shook hands with him as he leaned over the mourner's bench and beseeched me to give my heart to his God. I give it here. It appeared in the Oklahoma City *News*, on January 27, 1925.

"He is a very small potato." That was the reply of the Rev. Lincoln McConnell, First Baptist Church pastor. . . . "I have some doubt," said the Rev. McConnell, "as to whether I should feel honored or otherwise by the repeated mention of my name in this article by Herbert Asbury without realizing that this writer cannot possibly have inherited anything more from his illustrious ancestry than his name.

"I confess that it is rather surprising to me that editors of a magazine could attach enough importance to such cheap drivel as this as to give it the position and the space they do.

"The natural assumption is that they believe about religion, the religion of Christ, what this poor fellow does, and therefore, actually believe that this 'weak stuff' is a contribution to their cause.

"I remember Farmington, Mo., very well, having been there about twenty-five years ago. I do not remember Herbert Asbury at all.

"I am not surprised that I do not, as he must have been then somewhat as he evidently is now—a very small potato—and while I would feel naturally as interested in his conversion as in anyone else, at the same time I am forced to admit that it would not be possible for a man of training and experience to list a man of his evident mentality very highly, even though he were a professed convert in his meeting.

"I am very sorry that he was not really converted. If the Editor of the *American Mercury* cares for things of a really constructive nature, I can give him the life story of thousands of men and women whom because of the genuineness of their conversion to Christ in my own meetings, have given to the world characters of such beauty and worth as have reflected credit upon themselves and their church and have proved a blessing to society at large.

"I have never asked people to stand up if they want to go to Heaven. I think that very ridiculous."

6

IT was these people who taught me of God, and who had dominion over my spiritual welfare! And not only did they instruct me to worship their conception of Him; they threatened me with eternal damnation if I didn't, and with even more horrible punishment if I ventured to cast doubt upon the truth and holiness of the Bible. Eternal damnation meant that I should, in the life to come, hang throughout eternity on a revolving spit over a great fire in the deepest pit of Hell, while little red devils jabbed white-hot pokers into my quivering flesh and Satan stood by and curled his lip in glee. I received the impression that Satan was the only one actively concerned with religion who was ever permitted to laugh. God was not, nor His disciples, and that Satan could and apparently did was sufficient proof that laughter was wicked.

And they described God to me, and told me in minute

detail of the architectural design of Heaven and the fur-
nishings of the Mansions in the Sky. I do not know where
they obtained their information. I gathered that God was an
old man who wore a long white nightgown and boasted a lux-
uriant growth of whiskers, with a disposition compounded of
the snarls of a wounded wildcat and the pleasant conceits of
a *must* elephant. He chewed tobacco—perhaps that impression was due to the fact that so many of our preachers were
addicted to the vile weed—and He had an enormous head
which contained an eye for every person on earth, and this eye
was constantly upon its object. And it was a vindictive and
jaundiced eye, peering into the innermost depths of the soul
and the mind and the heart for some thought or feeling that
might call for punishment.

The descriptions of Heaven and the physical appearance
of the angels varied somewhat, according to whether the tale
was told by a preacher or a Brother, or a Sister. But all of
them talked with gusto of streets paved with gold and of
clouds lined with silver, of magnificent buildings constructed
of precious stones, and of angels sitting on the clouds with
no worthier purpose in life than strumming a golden harp,
protected from the weather by no more substantial raiment
than a white nightgown, a halo and a pair of sandals. And
whoever told the tale, there was always that underlying idea
of sybaritic magnificence; Heaven bore no resemblance to the
lowly stable in which the founder of their religion was born,
and it was not a somber retreat for the further development
of the soul and the cultivation of those virtues that are lost
sight of upon the earth. As it was described to me in my
youth, and as it is still described on those rare occasions when
I can bring myself to hold converse with a Preacher, Heaven
was a celestial reproduction of the palace of a Babylonian

monarch. Nobody worked, and God's House abounded with gold and silver and rubies and diamonds, and on every cloud that rolled down the street was a beautiful woman, eternally young and amiable. The Heaven that I was taught to aspire to was a motion picture set on an even grander scale than the creations of Cecil De Mille.

But even more emphasis was placed, in these tales, on feminine virginity. It seemed that Heaven was filled with virgins; I have never heard a Preacher describe an angel without mentioning the fact that the angel was a virgin, and I have never heard a Preacher describe Mary simply as the mother of Jesus. She is always the Virgin Mother, and he pronounces it all in capitals. Even as a boy I was impressed with the frequency with which the word "virgin" appeared in the discourses of our Pastor and in the lectures so freely bestowed upon me by the Brothers. It seemed to me that the word fascinated them; although I might be trembling with fear that God would strike me dead because I had not learned my Sunday-school lesson or had forgotten the Golden Text, I was so impressed that I found time to wonder at the enthusiasm with which they mouthed it.

It seemed impossible for Preachers or devout Brothers to say "virgin" as casually as they did other words; they gloated over it, toyed with it, rolled it about their tongues and tasted the full flavor of it before it slid drippingly from their lips with an amazing clarity of pronunciation. Usually they accompanied it with a doleful sigh. I thought then that the sigh was from excess of piety, and I thought that their eyes shone and their breath came a little faster from the same cause, that these things were possibly manifestations of God, and I was greatly impressed. But I am older now and I know better.

When I became old enough to understand what was meant

by virginity, and to understand that it was something more than a badge of the angels, I understood also many other things that had hitherto been mysteries. I knew then what was in the mind of one of the Brothers, an extraordinarily devout man with an astounding knowledge of the wishes of God and the manners and customs of Heaven, when he stopped me on the street one day and asked me what, if anything, had happened on a recent hay ride to Blumeyer's Ford and back by members of our social set.

"Did the boys and girls sit close together?" he asked.

"Yes, sir. We had to. We were on a hay wagon."

"Did you boys sit right up against them?"

I told him we did, and in my youthful innocence I remarked that I had been compelled to sit so close to one girl that we could hardly tell our legs apart. The old man drew a sharp breath, sighed and his eyes glistened. He repeated the word "legs" with gusto, he gloated over it, and then he said:

"You sat so close to her that your legs touched? Your leg touched hers? Your leg was right up against her?"

"Yes, sir. I had to."

"The leg of a young virgin!" mused the old devil. "That was wicked. It is wicked to think of the legs of a virgin. God will punish you."

He went away muttering to himself. I was disgusted, not at his ideas, because I had practically the same thought about virgins that he did, and so did most of the other boys of the town, but at his manner. Here was an old man who had set himself up as a mundane representative of the Lord, who told me whom to worship and how to worship Him, who held daily communion with God and received messages from Him touching on my conduct, gloating and trembling because a boy had sat with his leg against the leg of a girl in the forced confinement of a hay ride. God knows what is happening to him if he is alive in these days of short skirts and silk stockings.

Another of our Brothers, a very prominent member of one of our Protestant churches, kept a store in the business district not far from the Court House. He was waiting on a customer the day that the first woman to ride astride in our town cantered down Columbia Street, and his performance was a town scandal for many years. He caught a glimpse of the girl through the window, and he abandoned his customer and rushed to the street, in company with half the county officials who had been dozing with their feet on their desks, and all of the town loafers. The Brother followed her for several blocks, missing no detail of her costume, which was rather bizarre and daring for those days, and then he went back to his store and his customer.

He stood for a while wrapped in contemplation.

"She was riding like a man!" he said. "Her legs—her legs—"

My experiences in these matters, of course, were principally with Preachers and Brothers, but I had occasional contacts with the Sisters. They, too, described God and Heaven, but they did not conceive God as being quite so old and feeble as the Being worshipped by the Brothers, and for the most part they populated Heaven with handsome, stalwart young men, presumably virgins. I recall one exceedingly devout Sister who expressed the belief that there were no female angels in Heaven, and I have heard her praying with extraordinary fervor to God, in effect, to make an exception in her case. Whether she was justified in this optimistic opinion of herself I never knew, but I assume that she and the other Sisters, in their discussion of the virginity of angels, experienced the same sort of vicarious pleasure that seemed to mean so much to the Preachers and the Brothers.

7

I did not go to many camp meetings; ours was not a camp-meeting country. We went in more for protracted meetings, and for the stirring revivals of professional evangelists, held in comfortable church buildings. Usually I went to camp meeting only because some girl in whom I was interested had to go. But they were very popular with a certain type of young man about Farmington, who knew that religious emotion is very akin to secular emotion; the line of demarcation is very thin, and most men who have been around religious women very much know that one emotion can quickly be transformed into the other. Young girls are much easier prey after they have been overwhelmed by religion, their nerves upset and their brains whirling with emotion, and they are then easily persuaded that the Lord will forgive, even though His earthly agents will not. Of course such a statement could not be proven, but it is quite likely that more seductions have occurred at camp meetings, and *en route* to and from them, than on all the front porches and lawn swings that were ever manufactured, although in Farmington for many years a lawn swing was regarded as a lure of Hell. Even while the service was in progress the buggies around the meeting tent were filled with men and women petting, or, as we called it then, spooning.

Strange things happened at these camp meetings, and at the other gatherings as well, when a forthright religionist saw the light. At one such holy conclave an old woman, for many years a thorn in the flesh of the godly, suddenly bounced to her feet and shouted:

"Praise the Lord! My corn hurts! Praise the Lord!"

And this, because it embodied physical suffering and a great deal of mental torture as well, was accepted as an infallible sign that God had at last entered her soul. She had been converted, and all the rest of her life she was a prying, sanctimonious old pest. She used to stop me on the street and inquire as to the condition of my soul, and ask me whether I said my prayers at night, and whether I read the Bible, and she would grab me by the arm and pinch me and demand the Golden Text of the last Sunday-school lesson. And if by any chance I had forgotten or did not know, she scolded me and predicted dire things for me in the life to come. Incidentally, she knew all about the life to come; it seems that God had appeared to her in a vision, and had described Heaven to her.

At all of these meetings extraordinary efforts were made to ensnare the children and convert them to Christianity; the workers for the Lord were not at all concerned with the fact that the children did not know what it was all about, that they had no opportunity to choose their own religion, and with the further and obvious fact that they succumbed to nothing but fright and a great surge of emotion. That method persists. The Church still obtains its converts by noise and appeals to primitive emotion, and by threats, rather than by intelligently implanting a true and deep-seated conception of God and the heavenly wonders. But to the religionists a convert is a convert, no matter how obtained; I have known boys to be thrashed because they would not profess religion.

As with the Catholic Church, the unspoken and always denied slogan of the Methodists and of the other Protestant sects is "Catch 'em while they're young," but unlike the Catholics the Protestants cannot hold them. For one thing, they do not put on a good enough show; they do not understand lighting, and they have no uniforms and no Latin chanters. A Catholic priest covered by a surplice or what not, and his voice rising and falling sonorously in the chanting of a bit of Latin, is a very impressive spectacle, and his appearance lends dignity to his words. The gentle stare that most of them wear is also effective. As soon as an embryo Methodist becomes intelligent enough to visualize the sort of Heaven that the Brothers are preparing for him, he shudders and forthwith goes to the Devil, while the Catholics fill their converts with such fear of God and the Pope, or the Pope and God, to put them in the order of their importance, that very few get away. A renegade Catholic is almost as rare as a Methodist Preacher who does not think he is sprouting wings, and that his voice is truly the Voice of God.

CHAPTER V

A BAD BOY COMES TO JESUS

1

IT IS clear, then, that not only was my ancestral background religious, but that I lived in an atmosphere heavy with religious feeling. Religion and the Church dominated the whole of my early life. Among all of my relatives I do not recall one whose home was not oppressed, and whose life was not made miserable and fretful, by the terrible fear of a relentless God whose principal occupation seemed to be snooping about searching for someone to punish. Religion was poured down my throat in doses that strangled me and made me sick of soul. There was simply too much of it. God was fed to me morning, noon and night, and He did not taste good; I was hounded from pillar to post by a pack of baying, sanctimonious hypocrites beseeching me to get right with Jesus, and to read and believe that collection of Hebrew fairy tales called the Bible.

I came finally to think of God as I did of castor oil, and the flavor that He left in my mouth was just as frightful. He and His religion were personified by the dour-faced men and women who went sliding about the town; rubbing their hands together, scraping the skin from their souls but not from their palms. They were irritatingly gentle, and they sighed soulfully and mouthed platitudes with enormous gusto; they called each other Brother and Sister and poked their messy, prying fingers into every bit of fun that anybody tried to have; they fed their little shriveled souls with scandal and smeared dirt over everything that was amusing. They regarded all young men as professional seducers, and for the greater glory of God ruined the reputations of young girls who went buggy-riding and seemed to enjoy it—and nothing can be so completely and irrevocably ruined as the reputation of a young girl in a small town.

But despite the feelings of disgust and revolt which the labors of these servants of the Lord evoked in me, I did not definitely align myself on the side of the non-believers and the sinners until after I had been "converted." I began on that night to hate the Church and its religion, and all of its prying, messy hypocrisy and sanctimony. And especially I hated the preachers and the Brothers and Sisters. I still do; they give me a pain in the neck. I felt that I had been betrayed; I knew that the spirit of God was not working in me, but I was told that it was and dared to deny it. I was told that I must "get right with the Lord," whatever that may be.

I felt that the Brothers and Sisters and the evangelist had taken an unfair advantage of my emotions; there was a band at the revival, and under the influence of music I will do anything. It compelled me to do something that I did not want to do; it humiliated me in my own eyes, and nothing that has ever happened to me since has made me so miserable and ashamed.

I had reached the ripe old age of fourteen or fifteen when the hand of the Lord, operating through the agency of Brother McConnell and a horde of wailing Brothers and Sisters with religious fervor breaking out upon them like boils, reached out and plucked me from the burning. But it was not their fault that I had not been converted earlier; they had tried often enough. One of my earliest recollections is of a Preacher asking me why I did not profess religion and join the Church, and why I had not given my heart to God, as he called it. I was occasionally singled out at protracted meetings and at revivals and made the object of special prayers, but until Brother McConnell came with his improved technique and circus methods I had always held out.

2

MY own church, of course, was the Southern Methodist, but the revival meeting at which I was converted was a union gathering in the Northern Methodist edifice, which was about a block from Braun's saloon and an even shorter distance from the county jail. We called it the Rock church because it was constructed largely of granite blocks. Its members were considered good enough people in their way, but they were hardly among the socially elect, for many of them lived south of the Post Office among the Catholics and the Lutherans, and in some circles it was suspected that they held, at times, intercourse with the Devil. Nevertheless, they were Methodists and Christians and first-class politicians, and by this time they have probably assumed control of the town.

All of the Protestant congregations of Farmington chipped in to pay the $600 demanded by Brother McConnell for his week's work for the Lord. This was a goodly fee, but it was not considered exorbitant, as Brother McConnell was a professional devil-chaser with a national reputation, and it was felt that he, if anyone, could put Farmington on the right side of the heavenly ledger. There was considerable rivalry among our good people as to who should entertain the evangelist and pay for his fried chicken and other delicacies, and I do not recall who finally drew the plum. But the family whose bed and board he graced was considered very fortunate; it had practically assured itself of ultimate salvation, since the emissaries of the Devil would not dare to invade such a sanctuary of God.

Brother McConnell was an extraordinarily agile man. Throughout his service, and particularly after the collection had been taken up and found to be good, he bounded back and forth about the pulpit, chasing the Devil hither and yon, shaking his hair from his eyes, sweating at every pore and roaring charges about dens of evil that I, for one, was never able to find in Farmington, although I headed several exploring parties. He dealt largely in that sort of goods; to him, and to most of the other preachers that I recall, morality and goodness were nothing but chastity, and they never let an opportunity pass to insinuate that the finest men in our town whiled away their idle hours with scarlet women. Their insinuations, of course, had no basis in fact; to my knowledge there was but one professional scarlet woman in town, and there simply was not time. However, there were, to be sure, amateurs.

The church was crowded on the night I was told that Jesus had taken possession of my soul. I sat about the middle of the center section with my elder brother, a phlegmatic boy who was also converted but who would never talk much about it, while across the aisle were my sister and my younger brother. Every few moments the evangelist would stop shouting and sink back into his chair, gasping, wiping his brow and breaking into sobs as he bowed his head in a prayer that came in a throaty mumble from his lips. Here and there throughout the house was an echoing gasp and a strangled sob, utterances of tortured and frightened souls about to be swirled into a great wave of religious frenzy. And standing in the aisle and about the pulpit were Brothers and Sisters, experienced revival workers, eager retrievers for the Lord, their faces flushed with emotion and their eagle eyes roving the congregation in quest of just such persons.

The instant the evangelist sat down, his band leader popped up like a trained seal, and from the band and the augmented choir poured the lilting measures of a hymn.

Oh, that will be
Glory for me!
Glory for me,
Yes, glory for me!
 When by His grace
 I shall look on His face,
That will be glory,
Yes, glory for me!

The first hymn was usually something of this sort, a tune

with a swing to it, to get the congregation swaying in rhythm, and to attract the uncertain sinners lounging about the door and looking in, unable to decide whether or not to enter. Usually they came in after hearing "Glory" and a song or two like "Bringing in the Sheaves" and "Jesus, Lover of My Soul." Later the choir swung into the doleful songs like "Rock of Ages" and "Nearer, My God, to Thee." The emotional appeal was terrific; after the first hymn or two the audience joined, bellowing the words with fanatical fervor. Murmurs began to arise as the evangelist alternately talked and prayed, and then suddenly the music stopped, the preacher shut off his talk and for an instant there was a silence. It was theatrical hokum, but effective as always. Then Brother McConnell leaped and lunged to the front of the pulpit, his eyes glaring and his hair streaming down before his eyes. He flung his arms wide.

"Come to Jesus!" he shouted. "Brothers! Sisters! Come to Jesus!"

He stood there trembling, imploring the sinners to abandon their hellish lives, and the choir boomed into song:

> Lives there a friend like the lowly Jesus?
> No, not one!
> No, not one!

All over the church now there were cries of ecstatic agony as the victims writhed in emotional torture, and after a little while people began jumping to their feet and shouting:

"Glory! Glory to God! Hallelujah!"

The noise was deafening. People were shouting in every part of the audience, they were weeping and moaning. One old woman jumped to her feet, climbed onto her seat and began to yell:

"I see Jesus! I see Jesus! I see Jesus!"

She repeated it over and over again, "I see Jesus!" and finally, she collapsed into her seat, mumbling and weeping. The evangelist took up the cry. He roared back and forth across the pulpit, shaking his hands above his head, calling on God to damn the sinners. His whole body quivered and he screamed at the top of his voice:

"Jesus is in this house! Come to Jesus! Give your heart to God!"

And above the roar of his voice and the rumble of the seething congregation rose the music. It ebbed and flowed, it beat against the rafters and rebounded from the floor, always that regular beat of a hymn, like tomtoms in the jungles of Hayti. Many of the choir members sang hysterically, their voices rising on the high notes into veritable shrieks, but there was no change in the steady thunder of the organ or the wail of the violin, and there was no escaping the emotional effect of the song:

"Bringing in the sheaves,
Bringing in the sheaves,
We shall come rejoicing,
Bringing in the sheaves."

Then there was testimony. Old skinflints who had devoted their lives to cheating their neighbors, old women whose gossiping and backbiting were the talk of the town, hopped into the aisles and told how, at some previous meeting, God had entered their hearts and made them pure and holy. Their voices rose to shrieks; they grew red in the face from the fervor of their shouts, and one old man who had only that day cheated half a dozen men in a real-estate deal stood in the aisle with his hands raised toward Heaven and wept bitterly over the sins of the world. Tears streamed down their faces, and many who had only a few hours before dumped sand in the sugar groaned loudly in sympathetic torment, and shouted "Amen, Brother! Amen!"

By this time Brother McConnell's collar hung limp about his neck, but his passion for the Lord was unchecked. He stopped the testimony when it appeared that everybody in the church wanted to say something; there was another hymn and he began calling for converts. He shouted that we were all wicked sinners and must come to Jesus.

"All who want to go to Heaven stand up!"

Naturally, everybody stood up. He told them to sit down; they obeyed, for he held them in the hollow of his hand.

"All Christians stand up!"

Everybody stood up except my sister, and as I think things over after the lapse of years I know that was what first caused me to suspect that she was, and is, a remarkably intelligent woman. She said afterward that she resented Brother McConnell's holier-than-thou attitude, and thought he was an old windbag. She could not swallow his repeated assertion that he was a representative of God, and that the Lord had sent him to gather Farmington into the fold. She had, better than anyone else there, control over her emotions; she could not be stampeded. But for several years thereafter she was the target of a great deal of missionary zeal; even the Catholics tried their hands with her after it had become obvious that she would not subscribe to the beliefs of the Methodists, but all of it was unsuccessful. They could not feaze her even when they pointed her out as "that Asbury girl who wouldn't say she was a Christian."

Half the men and women in the church were sobbing while the band played, the choir sang its dismal tunes and Brother McConnell swayed back and forth in the pulpit and pleaded with them to get right with God and confess their sins.

"Oh, Brothers, come to Jesus!" he cried. "Let God enter your heart this night! Give your heart to Jesus!"

At the beginning of the moaning and groaning the Brothers and Sisters who were to act as procurers for the Lord scattered over the church, and as the services went on they picked out the ones who seemed to be most upset emotionally and therefore ripest for glory. They hung over these poor creatures, sniveling down their necks, exulting in their misery, exhorting them to march down the aisle and see God. These Brothers and Sisters, of course, had been converted many years before and were O.K. with the Lord.

"Oh, Brother!" they pleaded. "Come to glory! Give your heart to Jesus! Jesus died that you might be saved! He died on the cross for you! Brother, come to Jesus!"

And so on *ad nauseam*, with their continual repetition of Jesus and glory, glory and Jesus. There was no attempt at sensible argument, no effort to show the prospective converts that the Christian religion was better than the Mohammedan religion or the religion of Zoroaster; there was nothing but a continual hammering at emotional weaknesses. And finally the bewildered brains of the victims sagged under the strain and they stumbled into the aisles and were hauled and shoved and pushed down to the mourners' bench, and presumably into the presence of God as embodied in His earthly representative, Brother Lincoln McConnell.

■ ■ ■

3

I was fair game for them. There was hardly anybody in the church who did not know how emotional and how excitable I was, and how music affected me. Why, I used to be thrilled over the way I myself played the violin, and have been known to hang entranced over a tune of my own composition! Even before the services began I saw that many of the Brothers and Sisters had spotted me and were only waiting the proper moment to pounce upon me, and when the call for converts came as many of them as could get near me pleaded and begged and cajoled; they scrambled and almost fought in their eagerness to ensnare such a prime morsel for the Lord. They could have worked no more furiously if God had been keeping the score. They screeched at me that now was the time to see Jesus, that God was waiting impatiently for me to be converted.

Some of them even threatened. They painted horrible pictures of Hell; they told me that unless I went down the aisle and confessed my sins and asked God to forgive me I would sizzle and burn and scorch forevermore. One old woman, her face working with fanatical fury, screamed at me that I was holding up the salvation of my whole family; that my father and my mother and my sisters and brothers would not go to Heaven unless I professed religion; she shouted that Satan was waiting outside the church to lead me into the depths of Hell and light a fire under my immortal soul. The whole crew pushed and tugged and hauled at me; one Brother got hold of my arm and tried to drag me into the aisle, yelling "Come to Jesus! Jesus is calling for you!"

And up on the platform Brother McConnell was rampaging to and fro, working himself into a frenzy, shouting that "Jesus wants you!" and above the roar of the Christian workers and the moans of the victims rose the wailing whine of a violin played off key, the thunder of the organ and the emotion-filled voices of the choir.

> "Rock of Ages, cleft for me,
> Let me hide myself in thee!"

By this time I was crying; I did not want to go to Hell, and I was horribly afraid of the Devil, and I was not old enough to realize what was being done to me. Yet something kept telling me that I should not do this thing; that it was all a mockery and a fraud. I know now, and I knew soon after that night, that the music was what was the matter with me, not religion. I did not see Jesus, and I never have. It was that slow music; that doleful, wailing chant of the hymns. I couldn't withstand it. I never could. In the army I used to go to all of the funerals because I got such a terrific kick out of the funeral march and the sliding tramp of troops marching at half-step.

But I was doomed. It was in the cards that my self-respect was to be stripped from me and that I was to be emotionally butchered to make a religious holiday. They dragged and hauled at me until I was in the aisle, and then they got behind me and urged me forward. One old woman leaped ahead of us and performed a war dance that would have done credit to a frenzied worshiper of Voodoo. And as she pranced and cavorted she screamed:

"A bad boy is coming to Jesus!"

Others were going down too, shepherded by the hard-working Brothers and Sisters, and as they reached the bench Brother McConnell reached forward and grabbed their hands. For each one he shouted "Praise the Lord! Another sinner come to Jesus!" and then he gave the sinner an expert shove that catapulted him into the hands of a waiting Brother who immediately knelt with him and prayed. The team work was magnificent. I tried to hang back, but the band began playing again. The thunderous cadences of "Nearer, My God, to Thee," pealed from the organ, and I couldn't stand it. I was being torn to pieces emotionally, and I staggered and stumbled down the aisle, sobbing, hardly able to stand. They thought it was religion, and the Brothers and Sisters who were pushing and shoving me shouted ecstatically that God had me; it was obvious that I was suffering, and suffering has always been accepted as a true sign of holiness.

But it was not God and it was not religion. It was the music. Behind me came my brother, sedately, as he always did things. He went calmly to join the godly; for him there was no pushing and no pulling; when he saw me being dragged into the aisle he simply got to his feet and followed. I have always suspected that he went along merely to take care of me; frequently he did that. He was continually fighting my battles, and if he did not like the nicknames that the other boys fastened onto me, he protested so fiercely that the name was transferred to his shoulders. They tried to call me "Cat" for some obscure reason when I was a boy, and my brother did not like it; and to this day he is "Cat" Asbury in Farmington.

Brother McConnell grabbed my hand and shook it clammily when I reached the mourners' bench, and I was shoved into a seat. Immediately a Brother plopped down beside me, an old man whom I had known all my life, and who I knew perfectly well was an old skinflint and a hypocrite, a Sunday Christian. He put his arm around my shoulders and began to pray, crying down my neck and shouting that another soul had been saved, calling on the Lord to witness the good work that he was doing. I half expected him to say: "Give me credit, God; give me credit!" And all the time I was wishing to God that the band would stop playing; my nerves were being shattered by the constant and steady beat of the hymns, and the penetrating wail of the violin and the thunder of the organ.

And at last it did stop. There was silence in the church, except that here and there someone was writhing and moaning. But the shouting had ceased. Brother McConnell had his benches full, all of his workers had each a convert to work upon, and he decided to call it a day and save whatever sinners remained in the congregation for another night. So printed cards were passed around, which we were to sign, indicating the church we would join. Then the evangelist said for all of us who had been baptized to sit down. My brother and I sat down.

With no music to upset me I began to think, and the more I thought, the angrier I got. I was ashamed; I boiled with fury and I wanted to smash the Brothers and Sisters in their smug faces. But I was just a boy and I was afraid. It was at this point that my younger brother came down the aisle and tapped me on the shoulder.

"Hey!" he said. "Mary said to stand up; you haven't been baptized!"

"You tell her," I said, "to go to hell!"

Luckily none of the Brothers and Sisters heard me, so I escaped special prayers. I signed my card, agreeing to become a member of the Southern Methodist church, and soon afterward I was released. My sister and my two brothers went home, but I sneaked away and went down to the Post Office, where I found another boy whose influence with a bartender was sufficient to get us a drink. I went with him to a saloon not far from the old Grand Leader building, and there I had my first drink, a gin rickey, and when the bartender would not sell me another I gave a Negro cart-driver a half-dollar and he bought me a bottle of squirrel whisky which I consumed in the vacant lot behind the Odd Fellows' Hall. I got gloriously drunk, and about three o'clock in the morning I staggered home and up the stairs to the room which I shared with my brother. I awakened him, trying to undress, and he asked:

"What's the matter with you?"

"Hell's fire, Emmett!" I replied. "I've got religion."

I went to the preacher's house the next day so Brother Jenkins could sprinkle holy water upon my head and mumble a prayer, and later, having thus been baptized, I joined the church, but I joined with my tongue in my cheek and a sneer in my heart. I have never seen anything in any church since that would impel me to remove either my tongue or the sneer. And when I admitted publicly that I had been converted and was now a good and faithful servant of the Methodist God, I said to myself: "Over the left." That was our way of saying: "I am like hell!"

CHAPTER VI

NOTES ON A SAINTED RELATIVE

I

I WENT downtown the next morning after I had become a certified one hundred per cent convert, and was met by swarms of Brothers and Sisters who overwhelmed me with congratulations, and regaled me with tales of their own experiences when they saw God, and of the temptations that the Devil would now prepare for me. It seemed that I was not yet safe; I had, so far as they knew, accepted God and was one of His chosen children, although not a Jew, but He would still permit Satan to have his way with me upon occasion. I was instructed to walk humbly and with downcast eyes, not daring to look up lest I be led into sin. The Brothers, gloating the while, seemed especially anxious that the handsome young virgins of the town should not induce me to tread the scarlet paths of wickedness; the Sisters were more concerned with the Drink Demon, and the evils of playing cards and dancing. One Sister stopped me in front of Morris Brothers' store and, beating time with her hand, lifted her voice in song:

> "Yield not to temptation,
> For yielding is sin."

And so on.

Nearly all of them seemed to be obsessed by the conviction that at last I had done something to justify my ancestry; that Bishop Asbury had looked down from the Heavenly Mansions upon Brother McConnell's revival meeting and had approved the manner in which my conversion had been brought about.

"The Bishop is proud of you to-day, Herbie," said one devout Brother who sold shoddy clothing at high prices. "Last night was a great night for God and the Bishop."

I did not ask him how he knew that Bishop Asbury was proud of me, nor did I inquire into the source of his information that the conversion, by force, of a fourteen-year-old boy was a great thing for God. I merely said: "Yes, sir," and went my way. But it went on day after day; everybody in town, it seemed, had a word to say about the pride that now swelled the heart of the Bishop as he went about among the virgins of Heaven and lolled on a cloud strumming his golden harp and producing platinum and diamond music. I got very tired of it, and finally, to one old Sister who had apparently thought of nothing else for a week, I said:

"Oh, to hell with the Bishop!"

What blasphemy! She gasped and hurried away, and long before I reached home she had telephoned and told my mother that I had blasphemed and cried out against God. Naturally, my mother was worried; she thought from the tale told to her that I had gone up and down the streets of the town shouting defiance of God and yelling open praise of the Devil and all his works. But I told her the whole story, and she listened without comment, and when I had finished all she said was this:

"Well, don't say 'hell' to them."

I think that was the last I ever heard from my mother about religion, and from my father I heard even less. Once my mother asked me to read the Bible, and although of course I had already done so, I read it again. I read it twice, from the first absurdity of Genesis to the final fairy tale of Revelation. But I found nothing in it that caused me to believe that it was an inspired work, and nothing that proved, to me, the correctness of the pretensions so freely made by the Sisters and Brothers and the Preachers that they, and they alone, were the representatives and accredited agents of Jesus Christ on earth. And the sermons that I heard thereafter—the Preachers selected single verses from the Bible and constructed elaborate harangues around them—struck me more forcibly than ever as the trashiest sort of poppycock and balderdash. I was no longer afraid of the Hell that they pictured with such avidity, and I no longer thrilled to their tales of the magnificence of Heaven, although of course to a growing boy the presence of so many virgin angels, all apparently willing and available, was interesting. But none of them preached the religion of Christ; they preached hatred and revenge. They held out slight hope of reward; instead they were prophets of torture, promising eternal punishment for petty crimes.

2

IT was about this time, also, that I began to investigate the glories of Bishop Asbury, and to make such inquiries as I could into his saintly virtues. We had in our library the Bishop's Journals in three volumes, and we had also two or three volumes of biography, all of which I read. In later years I have read many others. Probably twenty or thirty books, in one form or another, have been written about Bishop Asbury, and I think that I have gone pretty thoroughly into most of them. But most of them are senseless if not downright idiotic; they were written by preachers and published by the Methodist Church, and the whole slant is religious. They are based on the assumption that a Preacher and a Bishop must of necessity be a holy man, and that all the little idiosyncrasies and faults that give a clue to the real character of the man, are but manifestations of the fight between God and Satan.

From an ecclesiastical point of view there can be no question of Bishop Asbury's greatness, for there have been few men who have left a more definite imprint on American religious culture. There were fewer than 500 Methodists in America when he came here in 1771; when he died there were 214,000, with good churches and great influence. He had completed the church organization according to his own ideas, ignoring to a large extent the plans of John Wesley as set forth by Thomas Rankin and Thomas Coke, and he had assumed as much power as a Pope of Rome. As a religious organizer he has had few equals, and it is a great pity that he did so much unnecessary organizing, and that his amazing genius should have flowered in such a futile and preposterous creation as the present-day Methodist Church; a great pity that he could not have developed a more flexible creed, one that would have grown as the world grew, instead of standing stock-still and viewing the universe with intolerant suspicion, with constant bickerings about the wishes of God and yelping appeals to the Almighty to damn somebody.

But statistically Bishop Asbury is even greater. He preached his first sermon in America at Philadelphia on the day he set foot on this continent, in October, 1771, and delivered his final pronouncement against sin on his deathbed, when, propped upon his pillows, he expounded the twenty-first chapter of Revelation. In these forty-five years he preached some 17,000 sermons, and probably 20,000 in his whole life, for he began preaching when he was about fifteen or sixteen, some three years after his conversion. The number of words that he uttered for the Lord is simply incalculable; there is no telling how far they would reach if they could be laid end to end.

In their methods of preaching and in their intolerance the preachers of my boyhood, of other sects as well as Methodists, were devout and faithful followers of Bishop Asbury. The bellowing evangelist of the Billy Sunday and Lincoln McConnell type is his lineal ecclesiastical descendant. He preached always at the top of his voice, for he had great faith in exhortation, and to him the good sermon was the noisy sermon; even today the Preacher who rants and raves is the one who is regarded by his flock as nearest to God.

When Bishop Asbury was not preaching he was praying; he rose every morning at four o'clock and prayed and read the Bible until six, when he breakfasted and set forth on his travels. He would not sleep more than six hours a night because Wesley had decided that six hours was enough. One day a week he fasted, and part of another day, punishing his flesh for the greater glory of the Lord.

This love of self-inflicted punishment affected his whole life. As a boy he was moody and sensitive; he appears to have been of the type that complains constantly that he is being "picked on." He was introspective, finding his greatest joy in self-pity, and he was never happy, as we used to say in Missouri, unless he was miserable. His playmates in the little English school near Birmingham called him "parson" because of his pious lugubriousness, and when the teacher beat him or something happened to cross him he sought solace in prayer.

References to his numerous physical ailments begin to appear in Bishop Asbury's Journals about 1772, when he was in his late twenties. He had never been strong physically, and never after he came to America was he in good health. He was apparently a hypochondriac, with all the hypochondriac's morbid delight in recounting his symptoms; many pages of his Journals are filled with them. He took enormous doses of medicine, performed slight surgical operations upon himself, and raised great blisters on the slightest provocation, frequently blistering his whole body from throat to abdomen. Once he preached a whole afternoon with so many blisters that he was not able either to stand or sit, for he had blistered not only the soles of his feet but less refined portions of his anatomy also; he had to be propped up in the pulpit, where he raved and ranted for hour after hour, saving many sinners.

He took no care of himself whatever, riding horseback through snowstorms and rainstorms with biting pains in his chest, and with his stomach and throat filled with ulcers, feverish from pain and religion.

All of these things he notes in his Journals with great gusto, and gives long lists of the medicines he took and the measures he employed to combat his sickness. Tartar emetic was his favorite remedy, and of this he swallowed enormous quantities. For an ulcerated throat he used a gargle of "sage tea, honey, vinegar and mustard, and after that another gargle of sage, tea, alum, rose leaves and loaf sugar to strengthen the parts." Another favorite remedy was a diet, as he called it, made from this remarkable formula: "one quart of hard cider, one hundred nails, a handful of snake root, a handful of pennell seed, a handful of wormwood." He boiled this concoction from a quart to a pint, and drank a wineglass of it each morning before breakfast for ten days, meanwhile using no butter, milk or meat. He notes in his Journal that "it will make the stomach very sick." It will. I brewed the drink once, and I had as soon drink dynamite; bootleg gin is nectar by comparison.

There can be little doubt that Bishop Asbury's physical condition had a great deal to do with his extraordinary piety, for it is true that most of the religious leaders have had many things wrong with their bodies, and that the sicker a man is, the more religious he is likely to be. A man who is healthy and normal mentally and physically seldom becomes fanatically religious. True, healthy men sometimes become monks and preachers, but except in rare instances such men are comparatively moderate in their views. And generally they do themselves very well in a material way, especially if they become monks.

It was once my journalistic duty to make a daily visit to a Franciscan monastery in Quincy, Illinois, and the good brothers remain a high light in a somewhat drab period. Jovial and pot-bellied, they were veritable Friar Tucks in brown bathrobes, extraordinarily hearty eaters and drinkers, and not even at pre-Volstead banquets have I ever received as much free food and drink as from the good Franciscans. It was easy to see why such men as these went in for religion, but it is not so easy to understand the motive of the Protestant minister. The earthly rewards are nothing to speak of, and what with evolution and one thing and another, he can no longer be certain that there is a Heaven to go to.

The Franciscans were fascinating spectacles as they padded on their sandaled feet through the gardens of the monastery and along the graveled paths that led to the church next door. I became particularly fond of Brother John—I think they called him Brother John, anyhow I did—who might have stepped from the pages of Boccaccio. He was the press representative of the monastery; he always answered my ring, and through the bars of the door I could see him waddling genially down the corridor, puffing and rattling his keys. It always seemed to me that Brother John was miscast; doubtless he lived a happy and carefree life, though perhaps overly cluttered with prayer, but I thought it a great pity that he could not have been an alderman. And what a bartender he would have made! His paunch would have elected him a City Father, and his fund of stories would have got him a job in any first-class barroom. But possibly he has reformed and is now leading some such useful life.

Brother John made but one effort to convert me and induce me to join the Catholic Church, and when I said "Bunk!" he stopped immediately and said that inasmuch as I would

undoubtedly go to Hell he would still take advantage of my
reportorial capacity to get a little publicity for the Church
before that unfortunate event occurred. But there was no tol-
erance in the attitude of my reverend relative, the Bishop. His
outstanding characteristic was intolerance; it shows in a hundred different acts of his career; he was arbitrary and domi-
neering. Anyone who was well dressed or who bore any
outward signs of prosperity was offensive in his sight; he
preached the gospel of poverty and self-denial, and believed
that all pleasure was wicked and that self-inflicted suffering
was heavenly bliss. He was imperious and scornful of restraint
and opposition; what he said was true he thought was true,
and that was all there was to it. When men differed with him
they were wrong, and he had no disposition to reopen any
question which he had once settled in his mind. He believed
that he was appointed by God to rule the Methodists in America, and that he was a legitimate successor of the Apostles. In
1801 he wrote:

"I will tell the world what I rest my authority on; first,
divine authority; second, seniority in America; third, the
election of the General Conference; fourth, my ordination by
Thomas Coke, Philip William Otterbein, Richard Whatcoat
and Thomas Vasey; fifth, because the signs of an Apostle
have been seen in me."

Divine authority and the signs of an Apostle!

Yet his steadfast belief that he was so appointed was one of
the secrets of his power and influence, which were greater than
that of any other churchman of his time. We are even yet feeling their effects, and we shall continue to feel them. There
seems to be no hope, what with Boards of Temperance, Prohibition and Public Morals and similar intolerant activities,

that the Methodist Church will ever become more worthy of respect than it was in his day. Indeed, it grows worse and worse.

Another prime factor in Bishop Asbury's extraordinary piety, as can be seen by the entries in his Journals and by a study of the biographies written by other clergymen, was his terrific mental turmoil. Throughout his whole life his mind whirled like a pinwheel; he was constantly in what, back in Missouri, we used to call a "terrible state." About the time he began to be ill he started referring to himself as "Poor Francis," and thereafter that was the dominant note of his life. He pitied himself because of his physical ills, and then dosed himself with horrid medicines, and with bleedings and blisterings, making his ailments more painful and himself an object of greater pity. He tortured himself thus physically, and flogged his mind with constant thoughts of his unworthiness; he was continually groveling before God, beseeching the Almighty to put temptation in his path. These extracts taken at random from his Journals show the trend of his thought:

"I do not sufficiently love God nor live by faith.

"I must lament that I am not perfectly crucified with God.

"I feel some conviction for sleeping too long.

"My heart is grieved and groaneth for want of more holiness.

"Unguarded and trivial conversation has brought a degree of spiritual deadness.

"My conscience reproves me for the appearance of levity.

"A cloud rested on my mind, which was occasioned by talking and jesting. I also feel at times tempted to impatience and pride of heart.

"My heart is still depressed for want of more religion.

"Were I to stand on my own merit, where should I go but to hell?

"Here I received a bitter pill from one of my greatest friends [referring to his last letter from John Wesley]. Praise the Lord for my trials also! May they be sanctified."

Bishop Asbury preached the same doctrine of personal conversion and sanctification that is preached by present-day Methodist ministers, and he sought this blissful state for himself with frenzied zealousness. At times he thought he had entered into what he called the full fruition of a life with God; at other times he fancied himself given up to Satan. The older he grew, the gloomier and more introspective he became, and like most of the other great religionists he had a pronounced streak of melancholia. He had alternating periods of exaltation and depression; he was either soaring the heights of religious ecstasy or floundering in the depths of sin and despair. He did not seem able to find any middle ground in which he could obtain a measure of peace and contentment; occasionally in his Journals he noted that he was happy in God and at peace, but the next entry showed him groaning in great vexation of spirit, crying out a doubt of the value of his religious life. He yearned for a constant religious thrill, and mourned because he could not satisfy his yearning.

CHAPTER VII

DIVERSIONS OF AN ABANDONED SINNER

1

ALMOST immediately after my conversion, or at least as soon as it had become noised about that I had consigned my holy relative to what some of our more finicky Sisters, unable to bring themselves to say "Hell," referred to coyly as "the bad place," I abandoned myself to a life of sin and became a total spiritual loss in the eyes of all Farmington except members of my immediate family and certain of my intimate friends who collaborated with me in various wicked but pleasant enterprises. That is to say, I cast aside the taboos and the inhibitions that religion had thrown about me, and became for the first time in my life a normal boy. I existed simply to play and raise hell generally, and for some curious reason the activity which gave me the most pleasure was throwing rocks at the church or in some manner interrupting the service.

It was not long before even the most hopeful had ceased their talk of sending me to a theological school and fitting me to carry on the family labors, for I began to smoke cigarettes, play cards, swear, drink when I could find a bartender willing to ignore the law forbidding the sale of liquor to a minor, and to cock an appreciative and appraising eye at the girls. It was then agreed that it was too late to do anything with me or for me, and on the Sunday morning that I mounted my new bicycle and rode brazenly past the Southern Methodist church as the Brothers and Sisters filed with bowed heads into the edifice for worship, I was consigned body and soul to the sizzling pits of Hell.

I suffered a great deal of physical agony before I learned to smoke cigarettes, and it was some time before I learned to blow smoke through my nose with the nonchalant ease affected by the group of older boys and young men who loafed in Doss's barber shop and around the Post Office Building and McKinney's peanut and popcorn machine. My older brother had learned a year or so before, and he frequently made himself very offensive to me by boasting that he could smoke a whole package of Sweet Caporals or Drums without becoming ill. I yearned to try, but he would not give me a cigarette, and neither would any of the other boys, and my finances were in such shape that I could not purchase any. And, of course, such wicked things could not be purchased and charged to my father; I could have charged a plug of chewing tobacco to him, but not cigarettes.

But one day I was loafing hopefully in McKinney's when

my brother came in and produced a dime that he had amassed by laborious work chopping wood at home, and bought a package of Sweet Caporal Little Cigars. These were really nothing but cigarettes wrapped with tobacco instead of paper, but they resembled a cigar and were thought to be infinitely more stylish and manly than the ordinary cigarette. I asked him for one, and he said he would not give one to John the Baptist himself. But I persisted, and followed him home, aghast at his determination to hide behind the barn and smoke the whole package one after the other.

"I'll light one from the end of the other," he boasted.

Finally as we came opposite Brother Nixon's house just south of Elmwood Seminary, he relented and very carefully opened the box and handed me a Little Cigar. It was a great moment. The yard of Elmwood Seminary fairly swarmed with girl students, including the young lady who at the time represented everything that was desirable in the female sex, and I visioned their cries of startled admiration as I passed, puffing nonchalantly, blowing smoke from my nose and perhaps from my ears.

I had no doubt of my ability to handle the innocent-looking Little Cigar; indeed, at that time I considered no problem insurmountable. My brother instructed me to fill my mouth with smoke and then take a long, deep breath, and after that blow the smoke out gently and slowly, holding the Little Cigar between the first and second finger and crooking the little finder as we did when we drank tea or coffee, that being a mark of gentility and refinement. As we came in front of the old Clardy homestead less than half a block from the Seminary I struck a match and applied it to the end of the Little Cigar, while my brother watched anxiously and from time to time gave me advice. I puffed as he directed.

"Got a mouthful?" he asked.

Unable to speak, my cheeks bulging, I nodded.

"Now take a long breath."

But, alas, I did not breathe; I swallowed, and while the smoke penetrated me and spread throughout my interior, it did not take the correct route. I began to strangle, and my brother got excited.

"Blow it out, you damn fool!" he cried. "You'll choke!"

I did choke. I did even worse; I became very ill, and the spectacle which so intrigued the young ladies of the Seminary that day was not that of a young gentleman going nonchalantly to Hell by the cigarette route. Instead, they saw a very sick boy rolling on the sidewalk trying desperately to stem a distressing internal upheaval.

It was several days later before I had enough courage to try again, and I debated within myself whether or not God had caused me to be so ill in order to show me that smoking was a sin. But I had definitely committed myself to the Devil, so a few days later I begged a dime from my father and bought a package of Drums and another of Sweet Caporals, the two most popular brands of cigarettes. With these, and a supply of matches, I went behind the barn. I made a neat pile of sawdust to lie upon, and there I remained the whole afternoon, smoking one cigarette after another. I was terribly ill at first, but gradually improved until the last three or four gave me no trouble. I did not have much appetite for dinner that night, but I had conquered the cigarette and I felt a glow of pride at the fact that I had got a very good start in the direction of the bad place.

The basis of my overwhelming desire to smoke cigarettes was the fact that cigarette-smoking when I was a boy in Farmington was one of the major sins. It ranked with adultery and just a little ahead of murder and theft. The Preachers called them coffin nails and delivered violent sermons against them, and every once in a while an evangelist would come to town with medical charts showing the effect of tobacco upon the interior human organs. But the fact that it was bad physically for growing boys was seldom stressed at all; we were impressed instead with the fact that God thought it a sin to smoke cigarettes, although it did not appear that it was a sin for the tobacconist to sell them. That was business.

Many efforts were made to reform me after I had begun to smoke. My mother said she had hoped I wouldn't, but that was all she said, and my father said he did not give a hoot whether I smoked or not, but that he hoped I would not be a fool and overdo it. He himself had learned the art of chewing tobacco when he was a boy of seven in Mississippi, and so far as I have ever been able to learn, God had never called him to account. He died at the age of seventy-nine, suddenly, and a slab of plug cut was in his pocket. It is impossible for me to believe that God refused him entrance into whatever Heaven there may be on account of his habit, which he thoroughly enjoyed.

But the Preachers and the Brothers and Sisters did not agree with my parents, nor would they admit that it was none of their business. On the contrary, they said that it was the Lord's business, and since they were the duly accredited agents of the Lord, appointed by Him to lead Farmington into the paths of righteousness, it was their business also. When Brother Fontaine was our Methodist pastor he did not look with disfavor upon chewing, because he himself was seldom without a chew and presumably had an indulgence from God, but he looked upon the cigarette as an invention of the Devil. In this view he was upheld by the Ladies' Aid Society and the Farmington branch of the Women's Christian Temperance Union. And the W. C. T. U., with the possible exception of the Methodist Board of Temperance, Prohibition and Public Morals, was and is the world's best example of an organization maintained for the sole purpose of minding other people's business.

The hullabaloo over my smoking only made me more determined to smoke until my insides turned black and I was called home by Satan and transformed into a tobacco demon. For that reason I probably smoked too much. As a matter of principle I always lighted a cigarette just in front of the Southern Methodist church, and in front of the home of my uncle, who was an enemy of anything that provided physical pleasure and contentment. I always smoked another as I passed the Northern Methodist church, the scene of the McConnell revival orgy, and still another in front of the Christian church, in memory of Brother Nations. That was four in half a mile, and of course was too many, but sometimes I was not permitted to finish all of them. Frequently a Brother or a Sister, seeing me thus flaunting my sin on the public highway, snatched the nasty thing from my mouth and gave me a lecture that dripped religion and was principally concerned with the fate of boys who defied God and Jesus Christ by smoking cigarettes. One sister asked me:

"Where did you get the vile things?"

I told her that I had bought them at her husband's store, and she shrieked:

"You saucy, blasphemous boy!"

But on that particular occasion I was not lectured, although she telephoned my mother that I had been impudent to her. My mother told her it was too bad.

2

I learned to play pinochle when I was about fifteen, only a few months after I had become an accomplished cigarette fiend and was generally considered a fine prospect for Satan, and thereafter was a regular participant in the game that went on every night in the back room of Karl Schliesser's cigar factory. This was a notable den of evil, and while religion had me in its clutches I thought black magic was practiced there, and that its habitués had communion with the Devil; among us it was believed that God had doubtless never heard of the place or He would have destroyed it with a withering blast of lightning. It was frequented by Germans and other low forms of life, and they were principally Catholics and Lutherans, with a sprinkling of renegade Protestants like myself. The Brothers and Sisters held the opinion that if this crowd had a God at all he must have been a very queer being, for bursts of ribald laughter came from Schliesser's back room, and there was card-playing, and I do not doubt that occasionally someone gambled.

Schliesser was the Town Socialist, and was looked upon with grave suspicion by the better element, as in those days it was generally recognized that a Socialist was an emissary of the Devil. But the Brothers and Sisters and the Preachers looked with even more suspicion upon Victor Quesnel. In this attitude they had the support of the Catholics. Victor Quesnel was born in France, but he had lived in Farmington for many years. He frequently quoted Voltaire, and appeared to believe that a man's religion and his belief or disbelief in God was a matter of his own personal taste, and he was therefore regarded as an atheist. As a matter of fact he was probably more truly religious than most of the pious Brothers and Sisters; the principal difference was that he did not try to compel everyone he met to embrace his creed.

Frequently, and without particular regard as to who heard him, Quesnel discussed the advantages of sleeping naked, or, as we say in present-day journalism, undraped. That was his hobby. He said he thought it was a healthful practice, that he slept better without clothing, and that come what might he was going to continue to sleep that way. This was considered heathenish doctrine; some of our finest church members owned stores in which they sold nightgowns and pajamas, and it was felt that Quesnel's attitude was not only a direct affront to God but was also injurious to business. Moreover, the Brothers and Sisters did not consider such a practice modest; there were scores, perhaps hundreds of people in Farmington who had never in their lives removed all of their clothing. Once at a meeting of the Ladies' Aid Society I heard an old Sister say that she had reached the age of sixty and had never been entirely undressed; and that when she bathed she kept her eyes closed as she applied the sponge to her body. A great deal of juicy conversation could be overheard at these Ladies' Aid meetings by a bright young lad who knew where the best keyholes were located.

3

SUNDAY was much more enjoyable after I had become a sinner and had left Sunday school and the Church to whatever fate the Lord had in store for them. I arose a little later, had a leisurely breakfast and a refreshing quarrel or fight with my brothers and sister, and then went leisurely to my room and as leisurely put on my Sunday suit, with no intention of removing it until I retired for the night. Curiously enough, as soon as I quit going regularly to church and Sunday school I began to wear my Sunday suit all day, and the little voice that I had in the selection of this garment I raised in hopeful pleas for loud checks and glaring colors. No longer did I wish to clothe myself in the sombre blacks suitable for church wear and religious activity; I desired to blossom and bloom in the more violent and pleasant colors of Hell.

Once arrayed in my Sunday suit, I left the house, a cigarette dangling from my lower lip, and my hat, carefully telescoped in the prevailing mode, sitting just so on the side of my head. I tried to time my march downtown so that I would reach Elmwood Seminary just as the young lady students resident there marched across the street, after Sunday school, from the Presbyterian church; they were not permitted to remain at the church during the fifteen or twenty-minute interval because they attracted such hordes of feverish boys intent upon everything but religion. Usually I reached the scene in time, and leaned nonchalantly against the Seminary fence, puffing vigorously and ostentatiously on a cigarette and winking at various and sundry of the girls as they passed in their caps and gowns.

For these smart-aleck activities I was presently placed upon the school's black list and was not permitted to call upon the one night each month allotted to such social intercourse, but as I soon learned to climb a rope ladder this did not annoy me greatly. Anyhow, calling night at Elmwood Seminary was not very exciting. The procedure was to place a dozen or so chairs about a big room, in pairs but with at least twelve inches between them, in which sat the girls and their callers. In the center sat a gimlet-eyed teacher, constantly ready with Biblical and other uplifting quotations and seeing to it that nothing scandalous occurred. From eight to ten the caller was permitted to engage his lady love in conversation, bet it was a rule that everything that was said must be audible to the teacher on guard. Whisperings and gigglings were taboo, and resulted in the young man being placed on the black list, and forbidden thereafter to darken the doors of the institution. But occasionally the teacher relaxed her vigilance for a moment, providing an opportunity to arrange a clandestine meeting. That was the principal reason that the boys of Farmington went to Elmwood on calling nights.

The regular Sunday incident of the Seminary girls having been brought to a satisfactory and successful conclusion, I went on downtown. I was very young then, and I considered myself, in my Sunday suit, a very striking and elegant figure. I thought of myself as a parade, and felt morally certain that the eyes of every girl were upon me, and that their hearts were fluttering with amatory admiration. The Methodist church was only two blocks south of the Presbyterian edifice, and I generally reached it as the Sunday-school pupils trooped out with their arms full of lesson pamphlets and their souls full of salvation, Golden Texts and catechisms. I regarded them pityingly, puffed vain-gloriously at my symbol of sin, and went on past the Christian church and the Northern Methodist church and so to McKinney's, the Post Office Building and the fascinating popcorn and peanut machine.

In the winter time Doss's barber shop was generally open until noon so Billy Priester could shine the shoes of the young bucks who proposed to defile the Sabbath by gallivanting around with young hussies. It was a favorite loafing place for all abandoned wretches who did not care for the glory that was free in all churches. But in summer we generally sat in front of McKinney's and the Post Office Building and, when finances permitted, ate popcorn and peanuts, envying Riley Hough as he hurried out now and then to attend to the machine and stuff his mouth with popcorn before hastening back into the store.

All of the young sinners of the town loafed there during the church services, and at twelve o'clock noon we rose in a body and walked down the street to Pelty's Book Store, where the Sunday papers were distributed. The afternoons were devoted to baseball games and amatory pursuits, and occasionally we went fishing. But this was considered a Cardinal Sin, and was frowned upon by even our liberal element; it was felt that it was a desecration of God's Day to drag one of His creatures from the river with a cruel fishhook. On week days, of course, fishing was all right, although a waste of time, but on Sunday an expedition to Blumeyer's Ford, or to Gruner's Hole, was followed the next morning by buzzing comment all over town, and only a grown man could hope to indulge in such sinful adventures and escape subsequent punishment.

4

IT was the custom of our pastors and pious brethren, and of the professional sorcerers who were imported from time to time to cast their spells and shoo the demons away from our housetops, to proclaim loudly and incessantly that our collective morals were compounded of a slice of Sodom and a cut of Gomorrah, with an extract of Babylon to flavor the sorry stew. They worried constantly and fretfully over our amorous activities; in their more feverish discourses appeared significant references to the great difficulty of remaining pure, and in effect they advised our young women to go armed to the teeth, prepared to do battle in defense of their virginity.

In Farmington and other small towns of the Middle West this sort of thing was the principal stock in trade of those who would lead their brethren to the worship of the current god; the evangelist assured his hearers that their town was overrun by harlots, and that brothels abounded in which prominent men abandoned themselves to shameful orgies, while church attendance dwindled, and collections became smaller and smaller, and chicken appeared less and less frequently upon the ministerial table. His tirades were generally in this fashion:

"Shall we permit these painted daughters of Jezebel, these bedizened hussies, to stalk the streets of this fair city and flaunt their sin in the face of the Lord? Shall we permit them to lure our sons and brothers into their vile haunts and ply their nefarious trade in the very shadow of the House of God? No! I say NO! Jesus Christ must live in this town!"

Immediately everyone shouted "Amen, Brother!" and "Praise the Lord!" But it was sometimes difficult to determine whether the congregation praised the Lord for inspiring the evangelist so courageously to defy the harlots, or for permitting him to discover them. If the Man of God could find them, why not the damned, too? Certainly there were always many who wondered if the brother had acquired any good addresses or telephone numbers since coming to town. Not infrequently, indeed, he was stealthily shadowed home by young men eager to settle this question.

These charges and denunciations were repeated, with trimmings, at the meetings for men only which were always a most interesting feature of the revivals. At similar gatherings for women, or ladies, as we called them in small-town journalism, his wife or a devout Sister discussed the question from the feminine viewpoint. What went on at these latter conclaves I do not know, though I can guess, for I have often seen young girls coming out of them giggling and blushing. The meetings for men were juicy, indeed. The evangelist discussed all angles of the subject, and in a very free manner. His own amorous exploits before he was converted were recited in considerable detail, and he painted vivid word pictures of the brothels he had visited, both as a paying client and in the course of his holy work. Almost invariably they were subterranean palaces hung with silks and satins, with soft rugs upon the floor, and filled with a vast multitude of handsome young women, all as loose as ashes. Having thus intimated, with some smirking, that for many years he was almost the sole support of harlotry, he became confidential. He leaned forward and said:

"There are such Dens of the Devil right here in your town!"

This was first-hand information, and immediately there was a stir in the audience, many of his hearers betraying an eagerness to be gone. But before they could get away the evangelist thundered:

"Shall we permit them to continue their wicked practices?"

I always hoped to be present some day when the audience forgot itself and answered that question with the thought that was so plainly in its mind, namely, "Yes!" But, alas, I never heard it, although there was much shouting of "Amen!" and "Glory to God!" These meetings for men only were generally held in the afternoon, and their net result was that the business of the drug store increased immediately, and when night fell bands of young good-for-nothings scurried hither and yon about the town, searching feverishly for the Dens of the Devil. They searched without fear, confident that modern science would save them from any untoward consequences, and knowing that no matter what they did they would go to Heaven if they permitted a preacher to intercede for them in the end, or a priest to sprinkle them with holy water.

But the Dens of the Devil were not found, neither in Farmington nor in any other small town in that region, for the very good reason that they did not exist. The evangelist did not know what he was talking about; he was simply using stock blather which he had found by experience would excite the weak-minded to both sexual and religious emotions. He knew that when they were thus upset they would be less likely to question his ravings—that they would be more pliable in his hands and easier to convert.

Our small towns were not overrun by harlots simply because harlotry could not flourish in a small town. It was economically impossible; there were not enough cash customers to make the scarlet career profitable. Also, the poor girls had to meet too much competition from emotional ladies who had the professional spirit but retained their amateur standing by various technicalities. And harlots, like the rest of us, had to live; they required the same sort of raiment and food that sufficed their virtuous sisters; it was not until they died that they wore nothing but the smoke of Hell and were able to subsist on a diet of brimstone and sulphur.

Many men who in larger communities would have patronized the professionals could not do so in a small town. They could not afford to; it was too dangerous. The moment a woman was suspected of being a harlot she was eagerly watched by everyone from the mayor down to the preachers, and the name of every man seen talking to her, or even looking at her, went winging swiftly from mouth to mouth, and was finally posted on the heavenly bulletin board as that of an immoral wretch. A house in which harlotry was practiced was picketed day and night by small boys eager to learn the forbidden mysteries, and by Brethren and Sisters hopefully sniffing for sin. It was not possible for a harlot to keep her clientele secret, for the sexual life of a small town is an open book, and news of amorous doings could not travel faster if each had a tabloid newspaper.

Exact statistics, of course, are not available, but it is probably true that no small American town has ever harbored a harlot whose income from professional services was sufficient to feed and clothe her. Few if any such towns have ever been the abode of more than one harlot at a time. When I was a boy every one had its town harlot, just as it had its town sot (this, of course, was before drunkards became extinct) and its town idiot. But she was generally a poor creature who was employed by day as a domestic servant and practiced her ancient art only in her hours of leisure. She turned to it partly for economic reasons, but chiefly because of a great yearning for human companionship, which she could obtain in no other way. She remained in it because she was almost instantly branded a Daughter of Satan, and shunned by good and bad alike. She seldom, if ever, realized that she was doing wrong; her moral standards were those of a bedbug. She thought of harlotry in terms of new ribbons and an occasional pair of shoes, and in terms of social intercourse; she was unmoral rather than immoral, and the proceeds of her profession, to her, were just so much extra spending money.

Small-town men who occasionally visited the larger cities, and there thought nothing of spending from ten to fifty dollars in metropolitan brothels, were very stingy in dealing with the town harlot. They considered a dollar an enormous price for her, and frequently they refused to give her anything. Many small communities were not able to support even a part-time harlot; consequently some members of the craft went from town to town, taking secular jobs and practicing harlotry as a side line until driven out by the godly, or until the inevitable business depression occurred. I recall one who made several towns along the O. K. Railroad in Northeastern Missouri as regularly as the shoe drummers. Her studio was always an empty box car on the town siding, and she had a mania for inscribing in such cars the exact dates and hours of her adventures, and her honoraria. It was not unusual to find in a car some such inscription as this:

"Ten P.M., July 8. Fifty cents."

These writings, scrawled in lead pencil or with a bit of chalk, were signed "Box Car Molly." Once, in a car from which I had unloaded many heavy bags of cement, I came across what seemed to be a pathetic bit of very early, and apparently authentic, Box-Car-Molliana. On the wall was this:

"I was ruined in this car May 10.

"BOX CAR MOLLY."

Our town harlot in Farmington was a scrawny creature called variously Fanny Fewclothes and Hatrack, but usually the latter in deference to her figure. When she stood with her arms outstretched she bore a remarkable resemblance to the tall hatracks then in general use in our homes, and since she was always most amiable and obliging, she was frequently asked to pose thus for the benefit of drummers and other infidels. In time, she came to take a considerable pride in this accomplishment; she referred to herself as a model, and talked vaguely of abandoning her wicked life and going to St. Louis, where she was sure she could make a living posing for artists.

Six days a week Hatrack was a competent and more or less virtuous drudge employed by one of our best families, but Sunday was her day off, and she then, in turn, offered her soul to the Lord and went to the Devil. For the latter purpose she utilized both the Masonic and Catholic cemeteries. Hatrack's regular Sunday-night parade, her descent from righteousness into sin, was one of the most fascinating events of the week, and promptly after supper those of us who did not have engagements to take young ladies to church (which was practically equivalent to publishing the banns) went downtown to the loafing place in front of the Post Office and waited impatiently.

On week days Hatrack turned a deaf ear to the blandishments of our roués, but on Sunday night she was more gracious. This, however, was not until she had gone to church and had been given to understand, tacitly but none the less clearly, that there was no room for her in the Kingdom of Heaven. Our Sunday-night services usually began about eight o'clock, following the meetings of the various young people's societies. At seven-thirty, regardless of the weather, the angular figure of Hatrack could be discerned coming down the hill from the direction of the cemeteries. She lived somewhere in that section and worked out by the day. She was always dressed in her best, and in her eyes was the light of a great resolve. She was going to church, and there was that in her walk and manner which said that thereafter she was going to lead a better life.

There was always a group of men waiting for her around

the Post Office. But although several muttered "Here she comes!" it was not good form to speak to her then, and she walked past them as if she had not seen them. But they, with their wide knowledge of the vagaries of the Agents of God, grinned hopefully and settled down to wait. They knew she would be back. She went on up the street past the Court House and turned into the Northern Methodist church, where she took a seat in the last row. All about her were empty seats; if they were not empty when she got there they were soon emptied. No one spoke to her. No one asked her to come to Jesus. No one held out a welcoming hand. No one prayed for her. No one offered her a hymn book. At the protracted meetings and revivals, which she invariably attended, none of the Brothers and Sisters tried to convert her; she was a Scarlet Woman and belonged to the Devil. There was no place for her in a respectable congregation. They could not afford to be seen talking to her, even in church, where God's love, by their theory, made brothers and sisters of us all.

It was pitiful to watch her; she listened to the Word with such rapt attention; she sang the hymns with such fanatical fervor, and she so yearned for the comforts of that barbaric religion and the blessings of easy intercourse with decent people. But she never got them. From the Christians and their God she got nothing but scorn. Of all the sinners in our town Hatrack would have been easiest to convert; she was so pathetically eager for salvation. If a Preacher, or a Brother, or a Sister, had so much as spoken a kind word to her she would have dropped to her knees and given up her soul to the Methodist God. And her conversion, in all likelihood, would have been permanent, for she was not mentally equipped for a struggle against the grandiose improbabilities of revealed religion. If someone had told her, as I was told, that God was an old man with long whiskers, she would not have called Him "Daddy," as some of her more flippant city sisters might have done; she would have accepted Him and gloried in Him.

But she was not plucked from the burning, for the workers for the Lord would have nothing to do with her, and by the end of the service her eyes had grown sullen and her lip had curled upward in a sneer. Before the final hymn was sung and the benediction pronounced upon the congregation, she got to her feet and left the church. None tried to stop her; she was not wanted in the House of God. I have seen her sit alone and miserably unhappy while the Preacher bellowed a sermon about forgiveness, with the whole church rocking to a chorus of sobbing, moaning amens as he told the stories of various Biblical harlots, and how God had forgiven them.

But for Hatrack there was no forgiveness. Mary Magdalene was a saint in Heaven, but Hatrack remained a harlot in Farmington. Every Sunday night for years she went through the same procedure. She was hopeful always that someone would speak to her and make a place for her, that the Brothers and Sisters who talked so volubly about the grace and the mercy of God would offer her some of the religion that they dripped so freely over everyone else in town. But they did not, and so she went back down the street to the Post Office, swishing her skirts and brazenly offering herself to all who desired her. The men who had been waiting for her, and who had known that she would come, leered at her and hailed her with obscene speech and gesture. And she gave them back leer for leer, meeting their sallies with giggles, and motioning with her head toward the cemeteries.

And so she went up the hill. A little while later a man left the group, remarking that he must go home. He followed her.

And a moment after that another left, and then another, until behind Hatrack was a line of men, about one to a block, who would not look at one another, and who looked sheepishly at the ground when they met anyone coming the other way. As each man accosted her in turn Hatrack inquired whether he was a Protestant or a Catholic. If he was a Protestant she took him into the Catholic cemetery; if he was a Catholic they went into the Masonic cemetery.

5

I fell a willing victim to the wiles of the Rum Demon on the night of my conversion, and thereafter, in common with other boys of the town who were aflame with revolt against the religious taboos which had so oppressed us, I drank whenever I could obtain the liquor. This was not often, because I seldom had any money and it was difficult to find a bartender who would sell a drink to a minor. The eagle eye of the W. C. T. U. was constantly upon him. But occasionally the darkies would buy for us in return for one swig at the bottle, and as often as possible we purchased by this means a pint or quart of whisky or gin. I did not drink because I liked the taste of liquor, for I didn't, and I do not now, but I thought it was smart and manly to get drunk.

And there was another, and a deeper reason. It seemed to me that in the eyes of the Preachers and the Brothers and Sisters a man could commit no more heinous sin than to get tight; it was even worse than smoking. Such being the case, I felt that it was incumbent upon me to achieve that condition, and thereby show them that I had no use for them and the things for which they stood. And that was also the reason we sang vulgar songs, and roared with gusto the parodies on hymns that we learned from time to time. It was our custom to get as drunk as possible and then group ourselves about the pump in the courthouse yard, where we bellowed ditties and parodies until the town marshal or some outraged Brother or Sister stopped us.

There were few such songs that we did not sing; it was at the pump, on a summer night, that I first heard the "Song of Jack Hall." It was taught to us by a shoe drummer from St. Louis, who sang it with appropriate gestures, and for a long time it was our favorite song. The version that we sang was this—it should be rendered with great gusto and feeling, and the final line of each verse should be dragged from deep down in the chest:

Oh, me nyme it is Jack Hall, 'tis Jack Hall,
Oh, me nyme it is Jack Hall, 'tis Jack Hall;
Oh, me nyme it is Jack Hall,
And I'll tell youse one and all,
The story of me fall,
    God damn your eyes.

Oh, I killed a man 'tis said, so 'tis said,
Oh, I killed a man 'tis said, so 'tis said;
Oh, I killed a man 'tis said,
And I kicked his bloody head,
And I left him lyin' dead,
    God damn his eyes.

So they chucked me here in quod, here in quod,
So they chucked me here in quod, here in quod;
So they chucked me here in quod,
With a bail and chain and rod,
They did, so help me God,

God damn their eyes.

Well, the parson be did come, he did come,
Well, the parson he did come, he did come;
Well, the parson he did come,
And he looked so God-damned glum,
As he talked of Kingdom Come,
    God damn his eyes.

And the sheriff he came, too, he came, too,
And the sheriff he came, too, he came, too;
And the sheriff he came, too,
With his little boys in blue,
He said: "Jack, we'll see you through,
    God damn your eyes."

So it's up the rope I go, up I go,
So it's up the rope I go, up I go;
So it's up the rope I go,
And those devils down below,
They'll say: "Jack, we told you so!"
    God damn their eyes.

The parodies on hymns that we sang were almost innumerable, and were undoubtedly sung all over the country by
other boys who, in the eyes of their elders, were only being
smart-alecky, but who, like us, had a deeper reason for the
eagerness with which they paraded their disrespect for the
Church and for religion. It was one of the few ways we knew
to flaunt our sin, and nothing pleased us more than to break
up a church service, or at least interrupt it, by bellowing at
the top of our voices some disreputable and unholy parody
that had reached us in one way or another.

One of our most enjoyable Sunday-night escapades was to
gather in a group outside a church window, and sing a parody

immediately after the choir and the congregation inside had sung the hymn itself. We persisted in this until finally the pastor of the Northern Methodist church had Wint Jackson, the Night Marshal, chase us away. We went without comment or objection when Jackson ordered us to disperse, because he had just killed a desperado named Yates, and we considered him something of a hero; we thought that he went about with his finger constantly in the trigger of his revolver, and that the finger itched.

On this particular night the parody which made the Methodist minister so angry, and swept from his mind all thought of his Christian duty to turn the other cheek for us to swat, was on "Oh, that will be glory for me." Our version went like this:

> Oh, there will be no chicken for me,
> No chicken for me, no chicken for me;
> When all the preachers have gulped their share,
> There'll be no chicken, no chicken for me.

To give the proper swing to the tune, "gulped" must be pronounced "gulluped."

Perhaps the most celebrated of all the parodies, at that time, was on the favorite old hymn, "At the Bar." We sang it thus:

> At the bar, at the bar,
> Where I smoked my first cigar,
>   And the nickels and the dimes rolled away;
> It was there, by chance,
> That I ripped my Sunday pants,
>   And now I can wear them every day.

Another parodied "Nearer, My God, to Thee," thus:

Nero, my dog, has fleas,
Nero has fleas;
     Although I wash him clean,
Nero, my dog, has fleas.

And thus, to the tune of "Hallelujah, Thine the Glory:

Hellilujah, I'm a hobo,
Hellilujah, I'm a bum;
Hellilujah, give us a handout,
Revive us again.

There was also in circulation at that time a great number of parodies on hymns in which mention was made of Beecham's Pills, the merits of which were emblazoned on every barn and fence throughout the countryside. I have heard that these parodies were circulated by the Beecham Pill people themselves in response to a plea of English churches for hymn books, but I do not know if the story is true. One of our favorites of this collection was the parody on "Hark, the herald angels sing." It went:

Hark, the herald Angels sing,
Beecham's Pills are just the thing;
Peace on earth and mercy mild,
Two for man and one for child.

6

TO my long list of unhallowed but frequently pleasant accomplishments I added, in my sixteenth summer, journalism and dancing; I went to work on the Farmington *Times* and learned to waltz and two-step, and on occasion danced the Virginia Reel and the quadrille with spirit and abandon if not with elegant grace. The practice of journalism was not then, in all quarters, considered a sin of the first magnitude; nor is it so considered to-day except when various Preachers and other goody-bodies find their names mentioned infrequently and their daily denunciations ignored. It is then the fashion to denounce the newspapers, and to deplore the low plane to which the fourth estate has fallen. But in Farmington in my youth the feeling against the Sunday newspaper was so great that it was felt generally that all journalism was at least slightly tainted, and so I list it as a sin. So far as the financial rewards go, it is even now nothing less than a crime.

There was no question about the sinfulness of dancing, especially the round dances, as we used to call the waltz and two-step. In some parts of the country exception was made for the square dances, but everywhere in my section of Missouri the waltz and two-step were considered Steps toward Hell. I frequently heard Preachers and Brothers and Sisters pronounce solemn judgment against young girls who indulged in such heinous practices, and brand them before God and man as abandoned scarlet women glorying in the unsanctified embraces of wicked men. That was the way the Preachers usually talked, too. One man in our town was even criticized for waltzing with his wife.

Not only was the wicked waltz and the devilish two-step, no matter how decorously performed, a Sunday taboo in our town, but in our most religious families it was taboo at all times, and several persons were dismissed from church for participating in such orgies. We had one Preacher who informed us that both Sodom and Gomorrah were destroyed by God because their inhabitants danced and for no other reason, and the prediction was freely made that Farmington was destined for the same dreadful end, and he intimated that we would not even reap the resultant benefits of great fame and publicity. His tirades were strikingly similar to the ones that are being made every day now by the Methodist Board of Temperance, Prohibition and Public Morals against New York City and other centers of sin.

As I have said, for many years the Presbyterians, city slickers at heart, had a virtual monopoly of dancing in Farmington. It was they who introduced the waltz and the two-step, to the great horror of all of our old women, both male and female, and it is they who must be held responsible when God sends His avenging angels to blast and destroy. Occasionally a Baptist or a Methodist backslid sufficiently to trip the light fantastic toe, as I delighted to call it as a juvenile reporter on the *Times*, but not often; generally the Presbyterians alone thus flaunted their wickedness. But when God failed to perform as expected, others became bold and abandoned all caution, and when I left Farmington, dancing was general and the town was obviously headed straight for Hell. But even then there was very little dancing done on Sunday night.

We had two newspapers in Farmington, the *Times* and the *News*, the former owned by Mr. Theodore Fisher and the latter by the Denman brothers, extraordinarily devout members of the Northern Methodist church and leaders in most of the town's religious activities. Mr. Fisher was a Presbyterian, a liberal at heart, but for business reasons he was unable to do or say anything to stem the tide of prying Puritanism. Both papers were controlled by the churches of the town, and published everything that the Preachers and the Brothers and

Sisters asked them to; as I grew older, Mr. Fisher became more confidential and frequently expressed his disgust at many things that went on in Farmington, but he was powerless. If he had said a word in favor of a more liberal attitude his paper would have had an even more difficult time getting along, and Heaven knows it was hard enough as it was; Mr. Fisher frequently had to spend all of Saturday morning collecting advertising accounts so he could pay wages in the afternoon. But the *News* was always very prosperous.

When I went into the newspaper business, or game, as it is called in the motion pictures and the schools of Journalism, I went in with the enthusiastic thoroughness with which I had abandoned myself to a life of sin. Mr. Fisher hired me at $2 a week, during the summer vacation, to be the office devil, and for that princely wage I built the fires each morning, swept the office, carried copy, set type, distributed pi, kicked the job press, cranked the gasoline engine on Thursdays, fed the big roller press, folded the papers, wrote names on them and carried them to the Post Office in sacks. And I had many other duties besides.

These multitudinous activities sufficed me for a few weeks, because in doing them, and in so being engaged in journalistic practice, I had the same feeling that so encouraged me when I danced or drank or smoked cigarettes; I was confident that I was doing something of which the righteous did not wholly approve. But later I became ambitious. I wanted to be an editor. Only God knows why, but I did. So I became an editor; indeed, I became many editors. Using the small job press and Mr. Fisher's stock of vari-colored inks, I printed cards informing the world that I was sporting editor, society editor, fire editor, crime editor, baseball editor, football editor, financial editor, religious editor, and barber-shop editor, this last because I purposed to interview the customers in Doss's barber shop.

Thus equipped, I felt able to handle any journalistic problem that might confront me, and I spent my spare time interviewing people and gathering items which, because of the extreme godliness of our citizens, usually consisted of nothing more exciting than announcements that so-and-so was on the sick list, or had been on the sick list and was now improving. When I asked a banker if he knew any news I gravely presented him with my financial-editor card; and when it became my proud duty to interview my youthful idol and our most famous citizen, Mr. Barney Pelty, the major-league baseball pitcher, he learned by ocular proof that I was both sporting editor and baseball editor, and as such fully competent to transmit to type and to posterity his deathless utterances. As I recall them, these were generally that he would be in town to visit his relatives or because some member of his family was on the sick list, and would then return to St. Louis to take up again the onerous duties of his profession. Once he predicted that the Browns would win the pennant, and I wrote this exclusive information with all the large and handsome words at my command, but he was mistaken.

As time went on I became almost everything that it was possible to be on the *Times;* I was printer, pressman, reporter, mechanic, editor of this and that, and what not. But I was never permitted to write editorials or chronicle the doings of our best people. The *Times* was passionately addicted to the Democrats, and each week our editorial page trumpeted the widely known and indisputable fact that the Republicans were a lot of skunks. These blasts were written,

and well written, by Mr. Fisher himself, and my own share in
the good work was merely to put them into type, and occasionally correct Mr. Fisher's phraseology when I did not think
that he had expressed himself clearly. And since these cor-
rections were made at the case after the proof had been corrected, they nearly always got printed, sometimes with dire
results. Once Mr. Fisher wrote, in jovial vein, about the gaudy
house in which a certain political candidate resided, and I
corrected it to read "bawdy house," holding that the latter
was more definitely descriptive.

Another member of Mr. Fisher's family, who had previ-
ously spoken to me pleasantly when she met me on the street
but who regarded me as nothing but hired help after I had
accepted employment, wrote about the social activities of our
first families on Columbia Street and the second and third
families in Doss's Addition. I was occasionally permitted to
describe the pitiful doings of the Catholics, the Lutherans
and other curious humans down near the ice plant, and the
weekly dances given by the abandoned young people at our
chief source of civic pride, the insane asylum. But the functions of Society were obviously beyond the descriptive pow-
ers of a mere printer's devil. It was bad enough that such a
person had to set the type. Nevertheless I attended these
functions, and gained great comfort by inserting my name in
the list of those present, and by adding the important and
vital information that dainty and delicious refreshments had
been served and a good time had by all. If it was a birthday
party the host was wished many happy returns of the day. It
was my belief at that time that it was against the law to pub-
lish an account of a social event without so stating. It was not
always true; frequently the refreshments were not delicious

and no one had a good time, but in those days I did not have that high regard for the truth that I have since acquired through labors on the great metropolitan journals; indeed, a night seldom passes now that I do not ask myself: "Have I written the truth to-day?" The answer, has, so far, eluded me. But Mr. Fisher, and to an even greater extent the Brothers Denman, sole owners of the *News*, frankly tried to please the advertisers and the subscribers; there was not then that fine spirit of independence which is such an essential part of modern journalism.

I advanced rapidly on the *Times*, and eventually was receiving $7 a week and had appointed myself to so many editorships that my cards filled two pockets. I was satisfied, and probably would have remained so for some years, but the end of my allotted time in Farmington was drawing near. I went to Northeast Missouri to visit relatives, and Mr. Fisher discharged me for overstaying my leave. This was a terrific blow; it seemed to me that my journalistic career had been cut off in the flower of its youth. I went to work in a lumber yard, and kept the job until the first carload of cement came in. But after I had pulled and tugged at the ninety-eight-pound sacks for ten hours I concluded that the lumber business held out no glowing promise for a young man who wished to retain his health and have leisure for a reasonable amount of traffic with Satan.

So I resigned and went to Quincy, Ill., where after considerable negotiations I obtained a job as reporter on the Quincy *Journal* and embarked on a career in daily journalism. So far this has kept me in the cities, where the opportunities for sin are vastly more numerous than in the small towns, but where there is less sin in proportion to the number of inhabitants.

This is true despite the horde of wailing prophets and professional devil-chasers and snoopers whose principal occupation is violent and false denunciation of every city large enough to have an electric-light plant. And in a city one can, by diligent search, find a few people who will admit that a man's religion, or his lack of religion, is his own affair.

CHAPTER VIII

CONCLUSIONS OF A MAN GONE TO THE DEVIL

IF THERE is anything in religious inheritance, or in the influence of a religious environment, I should be, if not an actual Pastor of a flock, at least one of the most devout of the faithful, a snooping Brother concerned only with good works. But instead of carrying on the work of my forefathers I find myself full of contempt for the Church, and disgust for the forms of religion. To me such things are silly; I cannot understand how grown people can believe in them, or how they can repress their giggles as they listen to the ministerial platitudes and perform such mummeries as are the rule in all churches.

Never since the night of my "conversion" have I gone into

a church to worship. I have frequently entered such dens of righteousness, but my visits, except for a few that I made soon after Brother McConnell's revival meeting to please my father and mother, have been on newspaper assignment or out of curiosity. I have inquired into the doctrine of almost every sect that has adherents in America, but in none of them have I been able to find any sign of a true and beneficent God. I can see only groups of sanctimonious, self-seeking Little Jack Horners chasing about poking their fingers into someone else's pie, and then shouting gleefully: "Look at me, God! Look what I found! Ooooh! Ain't it nice and smutty?" They cannot practice their religion without prancing and cavorting before the public eye; they are constantly showing off. They are not so much concerned with the glory of God as with the glory of the front page. And what time they are not whirling giddily in such imbecilities, they are engaged in disgusting squabbles among themselves as to who shall have the local agency for purveying religion; they want to copyright salvation in the name of their particular sect.

On all sides we hear that religion is the greatest thing in the world and that mankind's chief need is more of it. But it is my conviction that mankind would be infinitely better off with less of it, and probably best off with none of it. Nothing has ever caused more trouble. The whole history of religion is a record of war, murder, torture, rape, massacre, distrust, hypocrisy, anguish, persecution and continual and unseemly bickering; it is a rare church that has not been the scene of disorderly brawls. It has divided towns and nations into bitter factions; it has turned brother against sister and father against son; it has blighted romances; it is a prime cause of insanity; there is hardly anything harmful to the human race that it has not done as it pursued its meddlesome, intolerant way down the ages. Its followers proclaim loudly that their particular belief is synonymous with love, and bawl threats and epithets against anyone who denies it; but in truth religion comes more nearly to being synonymous with hatred and revenge, with each sect praying to God to grant it special privileges and to damn the others.

I have never at any time regretted my complete withdrawal from all forms of religion and churchly ceremony. During many years of my childhood, while mental and physical habits were forming, these things kept me in constant terror; I was horrified by the thought of the awful things that God was preparing to do to me; I was fearful and miserable lest I give birth to an idea that was not perfectly righteous and in keeping with His commands as laid down by His agents. The Bible, which I necessarily interpreted in the light of what I had been taught, caused me more nightmares than any other book I have ever read, and I was vastly more alarmed by the tales of the fires of Hell related to me by the Preachers and the Brothers and Sisters than I was in later life by the thunder of German artillery or the crackle of machine-gun bullets.

Since I left Farmington I have been near death many times, both as a soldier in France and from the natural ill-nesses incident to civil life. At least three times I have been told that I had but a few hours to live. Yet even then I did not feel the need of religion, nor for a preacher or a priest to pray over me to a God that neither of us knew, and perform cere-monies founded on pagan rites. How can an intelligent God pay any attention to a last-minute deathbed repentance that it is so obviously the result of fear and nothing else? The reli-gionist expects God to wash all his sins off the slate merely because, when he is about to die, he says he is sorry. If there be a God, cannot He look into such a shrunken little soul and see that there is nothing in it but a fear of death and a horror of the unknown?

I am not an atheist, because for all I know to the contrary there may be a God, or any number of Gods, but to me the God worshiped by my forefathers and by the religionists of to-day is a cruel, preposterous creation conceived by a people who felt the need of chastisement. He is a celestial traffic cop, hounded by whimpering weaklings who beseech Him to tell them they are on the right road, and yet keep trying to show Him which way the traffic should go. In the Christian and Jewish conceptions of the Heavenly Father I can see nothing that is fit for a civilized man to worship; indeed, the nearer a man approaches civilization and intelligence, the less need there is for him to worship anything. Conversely it is the stupid, illiterate man, knowing neither how to read nor how to think, who is most often the religious fanatic. He understands nothing and is afraid of everything; he goes through life as a small boy goes past a graveyard at night, whistling to keep up his courage. He requires religion and its twin, superstition, to give him strength to contemplate the wonders of the sunset and the falling rain.

For my part, I simply refuse to worry about God. If there is a God, I hope that I may in time find favor in His sight and obtain my share of the spiritual loot; there is nothing that I can do about it. And if there is no God, there is nothing I can do about that, either. I profess neither knowledge nor theory about the Supreme Being and the heavenly wonders; knowing nothing, I believe nothing, and believing nothing, I am prepared to believe anything, asking only reasonably correct information and authentic signs. These I fail to find in selfish prayers, constant squabbling over the wishes of the Lord and the building of magnificent temples within sight and hearing of the ramshackle tenements of the poor. I do not believe that I shall ever find them, for

"Wherefore and whence we are ye cannot know,
Nor where life springs, nor whither life doth go."

Without religion I thoroughly enjoy the business of living. I am oppressed by no dreadful taboos, and I am without fear; I set myself no standards save those of ordinary self-respect, decent consideration of the rights and privileges of others, and the observance of the laws of the land except Prohibition. To my own satisfaction, at least, I have proved that religion and the Church are not at all necessary to a full and happy life. And if I am thus a sinner and my chance of ultimate salvation forfeit, then the fault lies at the door of those fanatics whose method of teaching religion to a child was, and is, to hammer it into his head by constant threats of terrible punishment, by drawing torturing word pictures of Hell, by describing God as a vicious, vindictive old man, by scolding and tormenting and laying down taboos until the poor child's brain whirls in an agony of fright and misery. I know of no better way to salute them than to refer them to certain words of their own Savior, to be found in the thirty-fourth verse of the twenty-third chapter of the Book of St. Luke.

IF I ever have a son, which now seems unlikely, his boyhood will be quite different from my own. For him Sunday shall be a day of rest and pleasure; there shall be no taboos, and no attendance upon church and Sunday school unless their performances are more interesting than other available entertainment. They now rank just below the moving pictures, and are therefore last. I shall bring my son in contact with the sacred books of the Christians, the Jews, the Buddhists and of all the other religions as rapidly as he is able to comprehend them, and he shall be permitted to choose his own religion if he decides that a religion is necessary to his happiness and peace of mind. But if he shows any signs of becoming a preacher, priest or rabbi, or even a Brother, I shall whale hell out of him. I am that intolerant.

THE END